Contents

Illustrations	
Introduction	
1. The Manor of Barringtons, Chigwell	
2. Rolls Park in the 16th and 17th cent	
3. Eliab Harvey (1589–1661)	5
4. Sir Eliab Harvey (1635–1699)	5
5. Eliab Harvey (1659–1681)	7
6. William Harvey (1663–1731)	7
7. William Harvey (1689–1742)	8
8. William Harvey (1714–1763)	10
9. Eliab Harvey, KC, MP (1716–1769)	10
10. Edward Harvey (1718–1778)	12
11. William Harvey (1754–1779)	13
12. Rolls Park in the eighteenth century	13
13. Admiral Sir Eliab Harvey (1758–1830)	14
Early life	14
Parliamentary career 1780–1812	16
Naval career and Trafalgar Campaign	19
The *Temeraire*	23
Court-martial	25
Country squire and parliamentarian	27
14. Lady Louisa Harvey	30
15. Eliab and Louisa Harvey's family	31
16. Rolls Park in the nineteenth and early twentieth centuries	33
17. Life at Rolls Park in the 1920–1930s	34
18. The decline of Rolls Park 1939–1953	36
19. The Harvey family portraits	38
20. The Harvey monuments at Hempstead, Essex	42
21. Other Essex connections with Trafalgar	44
Bibliography	45
Notes	46
Appendix: Pedigree charts of the Harvey Family	48–49

Illustrations

Front cover – Rolls Park from J P Neale, *Seats of Noblemen and Gentlemen of England* (1827)

Inside front cover – Chigwell from Chapman and André Map 1777

[Between pages 26 and 27]

Plate 1 – Eliab Harvey (1589–1661)
Plate 2 – Mary Harvey (1607–1673)
Plate 3 – Sir Eliab Harvey (1635–1699)
Plate 4 – Lady Dorothy Harvey (1638–1725)
Plate 5 – William Harvey (1663–1731)
Plate 6 – Dorothy Harvey (1688–1711)
Plate 7 – William Harvey (1714–1763)
Plate 8 – Emma Harvey (1732–1767)
Plate 9 – Edward Harvey (1718–1778)
Plate 10 – Stephen Harvey (1757–1779)
Plate 11 – Admiral Sir Eliab Harvey (1758–1830)
Plate 12 – Admiral Sir Eliab Harvey: Hatchment in St Andrew's Church, Hempstead
Plate 13 – Battle of Trafalgar: Captain Harvey clearing the deck of the French and Spanish
Plate 14 – Battle of Trafalgar: Situation of the *Temeraire* at 3 pm, 21 October 1805
Plate 15 – *Temeraire* entering Portsmouth Harbour, December 1805
Plate 16 – The North-West Front, Rolls Park
Plate 17 – The Garden Front, Rolls Park
Plate 18 – The Stables, Rolls Park
Plate 19 – The Grand Staircase, Rolls Park
Plate 20 – The Music Room, Rolls Park, with the earliest group of portraits
Plate 21 – The Music Room, Rolls Park, with a family group by Sir Godfrey Kneller

Inside back cover – Map of Rolls Park Estate in 1894

Introduction

The Harvey family originally came from Folkestone in Kent, where, in 1578, William, the first of the seven sons of Thomas and Joane Harvey, was born. They also had two daughters. The fifth son was Eliab, born in 1589, and it appears that he or his brother, William, purchased an estate at Hempstead in Essex shortly before 1647. William Harvey was to become the celebrated physician who discovered the circulation of the blood. He seems to have spent little of his time in Essex and it was his brother Eliab, and his son, also Eliab, who purchased the manor of Barringtons and came to live at Rolls Park in Chigwell.

As was often the case in the seventeenth century, the success of many members of the Harvey family was founded on their interests in the City of London where the first Eliab (1589–1661) was a merchant trading with Turkey. In fact it is probable that Eliab came to Chigwell through his contact with Robert Abdy, John Chapman and Robert Abbott, who were also in the Levant trade and lived at Chigwell.

Eliab Harvey's son, Sir Eliab Harvey (1635–1699) was the first Harvey to come to prominence in Essex, where he was a Justice of the Peace, Deputy Lieutenant and MP. Succeeding generations were to follow similar paths in service to the local and county community over the next two hundred years. Rolls Park was within the legal limits of Waltham Forest, which consisted principally of Epping and Hainault Forests. The Harveys participated fully in the administration of the Forest with seven members of the family fulfilling the offices of either Master Keeper, Lieutenant, Verderer or Steward of the Court of Attachments from 1684 to 1830.

Much of the history of Essex has been shaped by the sea, and the Harvey family provided one of the heroes of Trafalgar when Captain Eliab Harvey (1758–1830), later to become Admiral Sir Eliab Harvey, commanded the *Temeraire* at the famous battle in 1805. Turner's well-known painting 'The Fighting *Temeraire*' can be seen in the National Gallery. Most heroes have a streak of eccentricity in them and, to judge from the letters of Eliab's wife, Louisa, to her eldest daughter, the Admiral was no exception.

The interior of the house at Rolls Park must have been one of the most richly decorated in the country in Georgian times. Fortunately a photographic record was made in 1918 before the sad decline of the house during and after the Second World War, which led to its demolition in 1953; only the orangery, stables and a cottage remaining. Part of the decoration of the house included many portraits of members of the family by well-known artists such as Sir Peter Lely, Sir Godfrey Kneller and Thomas Hudson. A number of the portraits have survived and remain in the ownership of descendants of the family, the Harveian Society of London, Galleries and private collectors. In the research for my book on the Verderers of Waltham Forest, I was privileged to be able to photograph thirteen of the portraits.

The Harvey family connection with the village of Hempstead, Essex, continues today. When the first Eliab Harvey was living at Winchlow Hall at Hempstead, he had built at the church of St Andrew the north chapel, above the Harvey vault. The chapel contains monuments to many of the distinguished members of the family, and the coffins of 49 Harveys lie in the vault below the chapel.

Other members of the descendants of Thomas and Joane Harvey, who did not live at Chigwell, achieved success in business, government service or in military careers. This booklet describes the careers and life of those members of the family who lived at Rolls Park, and in particular Admiral Sir Eliab Harvey, in this year of the 200th anniversary of the Battle of Trafalgar.

The photographs of portraits of members of the Harvey family are reproduced by kind permission of Lord Hamilton of Dalzell and the Harveian Society of London. The photographs of the interior and exterior of Rolls Park in 1918 are reproduced by permission of *Country Life*, and the illustrations of *Temeraire* at Trafalgar are reproduced by permission of the National Maritime Museum. I am most grateful to Nancy Edwards for her help and advice in researching the Harveys and Rolls Park. The extracts from the correspondence between John Strutt, MP, and Eliab Harvey (later Admiral Sir Eliab) are quoted by permission of Lord Rayleigh. The Essex Record Office, the National Archives (Public Record Office), the National Maritime Museum, Greenwich, the Royal Naval Museum, Portsmouth and the Loughton and Saffron Walden branches of Essex County Libraries, all provided invaluable sources of information. The portrait of Edward Harvey is reproduced by kind permission of the McManus Galleries, Dundee City Council Leisure and Arts.

The Society is indebted to Ted Martin for his time and skill in the production of the book

Loughton, February 2005   RICHARD MORRIS

1. The Manor of Barringtons, Chigwell

Chigwell Hall and Woolston are the only manors in Chigwell which can be traced back to Domesday. The history of Barringtons appears to start in the middle of the twelfth century, although it is not described as a manor until a century later. About 1135 Aubrey de Vere confirmed to Humphrey de Barinton a grant which he had previously made to his father Eustace de Barinton of his land at Chigwell. A grandson of Humphrey, Sir Nicholas de Barenton appears as lord of this manor on a fragment of a court roll dated 1249. The Barenton (Barrington) family held the manor in fee of the De Veres, Earls of Oxford, until the early part of the sixteenth century.

In 1563 the manor was sold by Thomas Barrington to Thomas Wiseman of Great Waltham, and passed to his son, Stephen, on his death a year later. A nephew, John Wiseman succeeded to the manor in the late 1570s and held it until his death in 1615. His son, Thomas, is said to have sold the manor in 1617 to John Hawkins, from whom it was sold to William Rolfe in 1626. The title to the manor passed again in 1629 to Henry Jackson who in 1630 and 1634 claimed forest rights in respect of the manor.

In 1639 Jackson sold for £1,900 the manor of Barringtons (alias Barrington) in Chigwell, with property in Loughton and Woodford, to Thomas Wilmer,[1] whose father had already being living for some years at Rolls, the mansion house of the manor. A court roll of the manor (1653) gives as lords Edmund Denny and Thomas Wilmer.[2] Wilmer had been a Major in the Royalist Army; and had probably sold half the manor to Denny to pay the fine for his delinquency. Financial difficulties led Wilmer in 1659 to sell all his land in Chigwell and a moiety of Barringtons to Robert Abdy of Albyns and John Chapman of London, with later a further moiety to Edmund Denny. Abdy and Chapman were apparently trustees for Robert Abbott of London, who made his will in 1657, leaving a moiety of Barringtons to his wife for life and in 1658 added a codicil leaving all his manors to his executors in trust to provide portions for his children. How he came into possession of this moiety is not disclosed, nor is he ever named as a lord in the court rolls. However, his brother-in-law was John Chapman.

Denny died in 1656, leaving his interest in the manor of Barringtons to his wife Anne. In 1657 the lords of Barringtons were Abdy, Chapman and Mrs Denny. Later in this year Anne married Francis Comyn. No deeds or other evidences have been found to show precisely how the manor was dealt with about this time. It is known, however, that Abbott, Chapman, Abdy and Eliab Harvey were all closely connected in the City, probably in the

Levant trade. Abbott died in 1658 and among the 'good friends' whom he named in his will were Mr Eliab Harvey the elder and Mr Robert Abdy. Eliab Harvey appears to have been living at Rolls, possibly as a tenant, for a few years before his death in 1661. In 1668 Abdy and Chapman sold half of the manor of Barringtons, with land in Chigwell, Woodford, Loughton and Waltham Holy Cross, to Sir Eliab Harvey (1635–1699, the eldest son of Eliab Harvey), and John Prestwood.[3]

Sir Eliab Harvey was named as joint lord of Barringtons with John Jakyll gent and John Berrisford gent from 1671 to 1691, with Berrisford alone in 1692, and with Francis Commings (Comyns) gent alone from 1695 to 1697. Probably Sir Eliab had bought out the mortgages in order to obtain possession of the manor within which stood the mansion which had become the family's country seat. Sir Eliab Harvey died in 1699 leaving all his manors in Essex to his eldest son William, who is named as lord of Barringtons jointly with Francis Comyns gent in the following August. From 1704 William Harvey (1663–1731) is shown in the court rolls as the sole lord of the manor, having in 1700 bought the moiety formerly held by Francis Comyns.[4]

2. Rolls Park in the sixteenth and seventeenth centuries

Rolls Park was the mansion house of the manor of Barringtons. There had been no doubt a house here from medieval times, at times occupied by members of the Barrington family, the early lords, but of this there is no direct evidence. In fact there is little information as to the occupiers before the seventeenth century. The subsidy of 1543 includes one Thomas Shelton gent near the head of the list.[5] He may have resided here, but no further reference to him has been found in Chigwell records; one Jone Shelton was a beneficiary under the will of Richard Cokke in 1504.[6] Later, the subsidies of 1599 and 1600 include one Guy Winnatt gent as a fairly substantial resident[7]; three of his children were baptised at Chigwell between 1591 and 1599 and both he and his wife, Joan, were buried at Chigwell in 1605. It must be admitted that it is pure conjecture whether these families lived at Rolls.

In the case of the 1628 subsidy[8] we are on safer ground, for it is known definitely that Thomas Wilmer who appears in that list, lived at Rolls, by which name the house was already known. He appears to have been here for at least six years earlier, for in 1622 the registers record the burial of James, son of Thomas Wilmer. His pedigree was registered in the Herald's Visitation of Essex in 1634 when he was described as of Chigwell and 'free of the Society of Salters, London'. He had been churchwarden in 1632. He was twice married. By his first wife, Elizabeth, daughter of Nicholas Gregory of Battersea, he had three sons, Thomas, Nicholas and Robert. In 1625 he married his second wife, Sarah, daughter of William Hodges of London, and by her had several daughters. He died in 1638 leaving all his lands worth £300 a year to his son Thomas and £500 to Nicholas. The Inquisition (*post mortem*) following his death was held at Stratford Langthorne and described Wilmer's lands in Chigwell as 'the tenement called Roles with the lands, tenements, woods, and orchard to the same pertaining in Chigwell in the County of Essex'.

Robert had died in 1623; Nicholas married Hester Clarkson in 1643 but died intestate within a month and was buried at Chigwell. Hester remarried one Robert Bagnall and was soon in conflict with her brother-in-law, Thomas Wilmer. She accused Thomas of arranging for Nicholas to be buried at Chigwell and for her to attend his burial there, during which time, so she said, Thomas entered her house and stole some bonds (and account books testifying to them) in which he stood bound, with a view to escaping payment.[9]

The younger Thomas, who was born in 1618, sold half of the manor of Barringtons but retained the mansion house of Rolls, which was the subject of his marriage settlement to his wife Mary.[10] As we have seen he was a Major in the Royalist Army and paid the penalty after its defeat. In 1648 he was ordered to submit a return of his properties, in which he declared, besides his London possessions and personal estate valued at £217, 'reall estate in Chigwell most in my owne occupation whereof Richard Goldson holds 26 li p Ann., worth £100'. He also said that he owed £400 on mortgage to Mr Nutt of Buntingford, whose brother William then lived at Monkhams. Although there was an order for the sequestration of his property, he was later able to come to terms with the Standing Committee for Essex appointed to fine and compound with the 'Delinquents in the Insurrection'. On the plea that he had to support his mother and four children, he was able to settle with a fine of £250 which enabled him to retain Rolls, among other property, although it seems that it was fairly heavily encumbered.[11]

It was probably financial stringency which compelled Wilmer to sell Rolls and all his land in Chigwell in 1659 to Robert Abdy and John Chapman, already joint lords of Barringtons. John Chapman, a city merchant, made Rolls his country residence, but with Eliab Harvey as a tenant in the latter years. He appears in the Hearth Tax return in 1666 with 17 hearths which made it then the largest house in the parish.[12]

It is likely that the site of the mansion at Rolls Park was originally occupied by a Tudor house, which was built of timber, no doubt in the style of the half-timber work of the period, but no traces of this house have been found. The Ordnance Survey map of 1894 shows the 'site of Barringtons' as approximately a quarter of a mile to the north-east of Rolls. The oldest part of the house that the Harveys inherited was the kitchen block in the centre of the house, built in about 1600, and late in the seventeenth century the north-east and north-west wings were built or rebuilt, making the plan L-shaped.[13] On the north-west side there were two late seventeenth-century chimney-stacks with pilasters at the angles.

Inside the building the kitchen had some original shelves with elaborately shaped and moulded framing carried down to the floor as arms to a former bench. The staircase in the kitchen wing had original square, moulded balusters, square newels with moulded tops and bases carved with roses, moulded strings and rails. The attic staircase had original flat shaped balusters.

Sir Eliab Harvey appears in the Hearth Tax return for 1670 with 24 hearths.[14] From this it is obvious he had already put in hand substantial alterations and extensions to the mansion. Late in 1667 Sir Eliab had a Royal Warrant to permit him to build outhouses for a dairy, corn-loft and pigeon-house, to make fish-ponds, and to enclose land to make bricks, etc near his mansion house called 'Rolles', and also to enclose Loughton Lane, leading from his house to Epping, on making another road as convenient instead.[15] This grant was confirmed three months later, when he was also given permission to 'construct' an apple orchard and to erect other buildings as he pleased.[16] The reason these grants were necessary was because the house was within the bounds of the Forest of Waltham, in which the Crown had certain rights. Thus in 1670 Sir Eliab submitted a petition for leave to disafforest his house and 170 acres adjoining in Chigwell, which though two miles distant from the unenclosed part was in the legal bounds of the Forest and subject to Forest laws. At the same time he asked for leave for himself and his servants to course, fly the hawk and shoot, on his lands.[17]

A photographic record of the interior of the mansion appeared in *Country Life* on 31 August 1918 and shows some of these original features (see the illustrations section). However, much of the history of the family in the text of the article is inaccurate, and was corrected in a later issue.

3. Eliab Harvey (1589–1661)

Eliab, the first of the Harveys to live at Rolls Park, became a successful merchant in the City of London, trading mainly with Turkey, and was admitted to the Grocers' Company in 1616. He had a town house in Broad Street, in the City, and country houses at Roehampton in Surrey, and Winchlow (Winslow) Hall near Hempstead in Essex, as well as Rolls Park. He owned other land at Great Sampford, Radwinter and Finchingfield in Essex and built the chapel in the north aisle of St Andrew's Church, Hempstead, with a vault below for the tombs of his descendants and their memorials in the chapel above.

Harvey was one of the wealthiest Royalists in the City, and sufficiently prominent for a reward to be offered for his capture in 1645. He escaped with a brief imprisonment and payment of £885.

It is likely that his brother, Dr Willam Harvey (1578–1657), the discoverer of the circulation of the blood, visited him rarely if ever at Chigwell. Eliab married Mary, daughter of Francis West of London. They had seven children, four sons and three daughters.

4. Sir Eliab Harvey (1635–1699)

The eldest son and heir, also called Eliab, was educated at Merchant Taylors' School, London. He continued the family tradition as a merchant trading with the Levant. In 1658 Eliab married Dorothy, daughter of Sir Thomas Whitmore, and they had eight children. Sir Eliab also had a town house, Cockaine House in Broad Street, in the City of London, and was fortunate that the Fire of London in 1666 is said to have stopped just short of his house.

In 1674 Harvey founded Folkestone Grammar School, Kent, from where his grandfather came. Sir Eliab was the first of eight Harveys to be appointed a Governor of Chigwell School, which office he held from 1669 until his death in 1699.

Sir Eliab was a man of considerable importance and was knighted in 1660. He was first elected Member of Parliament for Old Sarum, one of the old 'rotten boroughs', at a by-election in 1669 and became a very active member of the Cavalier Parliament. He was appointed to 149 committees, acted as teller in 23 divisions and made 44 recorded speeches. He was the first merchant, with no more than a primary education, to achieve prominence in debate from the opposition benches during the Cavalier Parliament. Harvey was returned for the County of Essex unopposed at the first General Election in March 1679, but lost his seat at the next election and had subsequently to seek re-election for his old seat at Old Sarum, which he represented in 1679, 1681 and 1685. A staunch Tory he did not stand again until 1693 when he became the Member for Maldon, which seat he retained until his death in 1699.

Harvey's sober godliness and anti-popery had made him an active member of the so called 'Country' group of MPs in the reign of Charles II, but he seems to have been won over during James II's campaign to enlist the support of Dissenters or their allies, hosting a dinner for the King in June 1688. In 1689, after the Glorious Revolution, he was listed among other former Country party MPs as one of those 'eminent in Parliament, useful men, but not to be trusted'.

In the 1695 Parliament he was listed as a probable opponent of the government on the proposed council of trade, and refused to sign the Association in February 1696. If this obstinacy is to be construed as evidence of Jacobite sympathies, it is worth noting that he was not deprived of his 'very considerable command' as Lieutenant of Waltham Forest, and that his third son, Matthew, was first page of honour to William III.[18]

Rolls was no doubt a fitting residence for a man of his standing and there is evidence that he was frequently in residence. In 1681 he was present at a survey made in connection with the churchyard fence, and in 1684 the burial is recorded of Mr Deboe, a Frenchman who died at Sir Eliab Harvey's.

He was a Justice of the Peace and a Deputy Lieutenant for Essex. In about 1684 he was appointed Lieutenant of Waltham Forest. In June 1684 concern about illegal hunting in the Forest led the Chief Justice of all the forests south of the Trent, the Earl of Chesterfield, to write to Sir Eliab Harvey, as Lieutenant of the Forest and the Keepers and Purlieu Rangers of the Forest. In his letter, the Chief Justice complained that various people were entering the Forest with packs of hounds to hunt foxes and hares, thereby driving His Majesty's deer from their quiet feed and Layer, and forcing them out into the adjoining open country where they did much damage to the farmers' crops, before being killed by the poachers. The Chief Justice instructed the Keepers and Purlieu Rangers to catch the poachers and to bring them before the courts. Chesterfield ended by requiring Sir Eliab Harvey to read and publish the letter to all the Forest officers, and to make it clear to them that failure to enforce the Forest laws would be at their own peril![19]

Sir Eliab Harvey died in 1699 and was buried in the family vault at

Hempstead: 'much lamented, being a gentleman of an extraordinary good character.'

5. Eliab Harvey 1659–1681

Sir Eliab Harvey's eldest son, also called Eliab, was baptised on 2 November 1659, at the church of St Peter-le-Poor, in the City of London. He was educated at Christ Church, Oxford, and in November 1680 he married Dorothy, daughter of Sir Robert Dycer, 2nd Baronet of Hackney, Middlesex, a twelve-year old heiress.

Harvey was elected Member of Parliament for Old Sarum in March 1679, under age, on his father's interest. He was marked 'honest' on Shaftesbury's list, but was named to no committees and made no speeches. He never stood again, as the seat was required for his father in the second and third Exclusion Parliaments. He was admitted to the Freedom of the City of Salisbury, with his father, in January 1679.

He died on 3 June 1681, at the age of 22, and was buried at Hempstead. The ecclesiastical court found that his marriage to Dorothy Dycer had not been consummated, and the widow married her brother-in-law, William, three months later.

6. William Harvey (1663–1731)

As Sir Eliab's eldest son, Eliab, had died in June 1681, Rolls came to his second son, William, who had married his late brother's wife, Dorothy, in September 1681. William was then only 18, but the Harveys were obviously not ready to let such a fortune slip. Dorothy's first child was born on 12 March 1684, two months before her sixteenth birthday. She had all her six children before her twenty-fourth birthday and was a grandmother when she died aged 43.

William, who had been educated at St Paul's School, went up to Trinity College, Cambridge, in 1680, and was presumably still an undergraduate at the time of his marriage. He was appointed a Governor of Chigwell School in 1683. From 1704 William Harvey is shown in the court rolls as the sole lord of the manor of Barringtons, having in 1700 bought the moiety formerly held by Francis Comyn.

William Harvey was a Tory country gentleman with an income of

£5,000–£6,000 a year. He first entered Parliament as the Member for Old Sarum, Wiltshire, from 1689–1705. In 1705 he was elected as the Member for Appleby, but at the election in 1708 he was again returned for Old Sarum. He was elected the member for Weymouth in the Parliament of 1711–1713, and for Melcombe Regis in the Parliament of 1714–1715. Harvey was returned in 1715 at a by-election for the County of Essex, after contesting Bridport unsuccessfully. Re-elected for Essex in 1722, he did not stand in 1727.

Despite having inherited a considerable estate, Harvey may have experienced financial problems in about 1713, as, in May of that year, he secured the passage of a private Bill in Parliament enabling him to sell off lands in Suffolk to provide portions for his daughters and a jointure of £1,200 in anticipation of his son's marriage, and in later years he was forced to sell further property in Roehampton. He continued to sit in Parliament after 1715 and was regarded by some as a Jacobite.[20]

He was, nevertheless, active in local affairs, being Master Keeper of Lambourne and Chigwell Walks in Waltham Forest from 1713 and Lieutenant of the Forest from 1719 until his death.[21] In 1708 he was one of the local justices appointed to report as to whether Loughton Bridge, which was then in a bad state of repair, was a charge on the county or the parish.[22] In 1713 he sought a licence from the Court of Attachments to fell Barrington's Grove of nine acres.

William Harvey signed his attendance at Vestry meetings in 1724 and 1728, but this may well have been his son. He died in 1731 at the age of 68. He also had a son, Eliab, who predeceased him.

7. William Harvey (1689–1742)

William's eldest surviving son, also called William, was born in 1689. During the lifetime of his father he was already active in local affairs and in 1714 became Master Keeper of Loughton Walk. He married Mary, daughter and co-heiress of Ralph Williamson Esq of Berwick. Soon after his father's death, in 1733, he was appointed Sheriff of Essex and in 1738 he was elected a Verderer of Waltham Forest in place of Sir Henry Maynard who had died.

At the Court of Attachments held at the King's Head, Chigwell, on 26 May 1739, Harvey was sworn in as a Verderer. One of the presentments that day was a request from Richard Salway of Woodford, a merchant trading with Turkey and the Levant, to shoot, hunt and fish in the Forest, except of course deer. It is possible that Harvey knew Salway from their mutual interests in trade in the City. Harvey remained Master Keeper of Loughton Walk while he was a Verderer.

Elected Member of Parliament for Old Sarum in 1710, Harvey was classed as a Tory. A member of the October Club, he was included in the 1710–1711 session among the 'worthy patriots' who had helped to detect the mismanagement of the previous administration. Unsuccessful for Old Sarum in 1713, he did not stand again for Parliament.[23]

It is surprising that he also took a parish office – Surveyor of the Highways for the Manor of Barringtons – from 1733 until his death. It is not likely that he dealt with the day-to-day administration, but there can be no doubt that his position enabled him to enforce his tenants and copyholds to supply the statutory labour for the repair of the highways, rather more forcefully than lesser ratepayers could.[24]

In 1734 an enquiry was held to consider his application to alter the course of the public road adjoining Rolls.[25] It seems that the junction of the road from Chigwell Street to Abridge and the road to Loughton Bridge was then some two hundred yards nearer Chigwell village. This petition enabled him to extend the grounds surrounding the house and to build more extensive stables. It was probably at this time that the high brick wall, which stands now by the Abridge Road, was built. William would have kept a large staff at Rolls; the burials of at least two of his servants are recorded in the Chigwell registers, Richard Lambert in 1737 and Jonathan Jaren in 1738.

In April 1741 Sir John Eyles, Carew Hervey Mildmay and William Harvey presided at the Court of Attachments. Edward Skingle had presented a petition to the Verderers requesting that he be granted half an acre of waste ground lying in Walthamstow Walk, on which to erect a cottage. The petition had been signed by Lord and Lady Maynard, the lord and lady of the manor, and by most of the principal inhabitants of the manor. The court agreed that the cottage could be built in a convenient place, provided it was not prejudicial to His Majesty's Vert or Venison.

Harvey lived for the early part of his married life at Winchlow Hall at Hempstead, but from at least 1723 he resided at Chigwell.[26] William and Mary had three sons and two daughters and, on William's death at Rolls in 1742 at the age of only 54, he was succeeded by his eldest son, also called William. He was buried at Hempstead.

8. William Harvey (1714–1763)

Born in June 1714, William, like his father, continued the office of Surveyor of the Highways. In 1750 he married at Walthamstow, Emma, daughter and heiress of Stephen Skynner of Leytonstone, which marriage brought certain additional estates to the Harvey family. They had nine children: five sons and four daughters, several of whom were baptised at Chigwell. He became a Governor of Chigwell School in 1733.

In February 1743 William was elected a Verderer of Waltham Forest. In 1750 he became a Governor of St Bartholomew's Hospital, donating £50 towards the cost of the new buildings.[27] In 1756 he received the honorary degree of DCL at Cambridge and in 1758 was appointed a Deputy Lieutenant for the County of Essex.

Harvey was elected as the Member of Parliament for Essex in 1747 and was returned at the elections in 1754 and 1761. In all cases his election was unopposed and he was invariably classed as a Tory. While himself an independent country gentleman, Harvey was seeking promotion for his brothers: he tried to have Eliab made a KC, and was offended when a junior barrister was preferred. However, Eliab later received silk. His other brother, Edward, who had pursued a military career, is said to have secured promotion as a result of William's influence. There is no record of Harvey having spoken in the House.

He was Colonel of the Western Battalion of the Essex Militia but fought with the Jacobites in Prince Charles Edward's army at the Battle of Culloden in 1746. When the rebellion was eventually subdued, William narrowly escaped the extreme penalty for his loyalty to Charles, and it was only through the intervention of his brother, Edward, that he was freed.

He died in 1763 and was buried at Hempstead. William Harvey described himself as an independent country gentleman. This was reflected in the circumstances of his death: 'Will Harvey died on an apoplexy at Wanstead. He had hunted in the morning, and was in a boat in the water, talking to Mr G Greville, when he was taken speechless, and expired presently.'[28]

9. Eliab Harvey, KC, MP (1716–1769)

Eliab Harvey was the second son of William and Mary Harvey. Born at Chigwell on 23 May 1716, he was educated at Westminster School, where he became a King's Scholar, and at Trinity College, Cambridge, where he was elected a Fellow in 1740. Eliab was admitted to the Inner Temple in May 1733 and called to the Bar in June 1741 and was appointed a KC in 1758. He followed the family tradition and was appointed a Governor of Chigwell School in 1747 and in 1763, he was appointed Steward of the Court of Attachments of Waltham Forest. A year later Harvey was honoured by his election as a Fellow of the Royal Society. The citation for his election reads:

> Eliab Harvey Esqr.
> of Lincoln's Inn fields, member of parliament, & one of his majesty's council [sic], learned in the law,
> a gentleman of great merit & learning, & a zealous promoter of useful knowledge, being desirous of becoming a fellow of the royal Society, is recom[m]ended by us upon our own acquaintance with him as highly deserving the honour he desires.
> Proposers: Willoughby, Geo Eckersall, Tho Birch, James Burrow, Owen Salusbury Brereton, Saml Wegg, William Man Godschall. Balloted for & Elected 29 March 1764.
> Admitted 12 April 1764.[29]

The circumstances of Harvey entering Parliament in 1761, as the Member for Dunwich, were somewhat unusual. He was offered the seat subject to his brother, Edward, keeping his seat at Midhurst. If not, Eliab was to allow Edward to stand for Dunwich. When a compromise at Midhurst left Edward without a seat, Eliab was offered the chief justiceship of Ireland in lieu of Dunwich, with a peerage and head of the law in Ireland likely to come later. However, Eliab decided that he did not wish to leave England, and rejected the proposal and insisted on standing at Dunwich. He was returned unopposed and Edward was left without a seat.

Harvey was a frequent speaker on a diversity of subjects and James Harris noted that as a speaker he had 'force and precision'. He did not stand again for Dunwich in 1768, the interest there no longer being at the disposal of the government. He was nominated for Essex at a meeting of country gentlemen discontented with the sitting Members, but came bottom of the poll.

In November 1756 Eliab married Mary, daughter of Richard Benyon of Gidea Hall, near Romford, Essex. They had three sons and two daughters. The first two sons, Eliab and Richard predeceased their father. The third son, Edward (b 1765) died in 1784, fifteen years after his father's death, but before reaching his majority, and as a result the surviving daughter, Elizabeth became Eliab's heir. In 1780 she married Montagu Burgoyne. The

Burgoynes were well known in the social circle of the Harveys, although Burgoyne's political views (Whig) differed considerably from the Tory Harveys.

In 1767 Eliab Harvey purchased from John Goodere the mansion and estate of Claybury Hall, near Woodford Bridge. However, Eliab and Mary may have been living in the house as a tenant from 1753. Eliab's heir, Elizabeth, and her husband Montagu Burgoyne, sold the house and estate to James Hatch in 1786, which at this time covered approximately 160 acres. Eliab also owned a considerable amount of land in other parts of south-west Essex, including the Monkhams estate in Woodford, which he purchased from Thomas Cox North in 1760. Harvey's executors sold the estate in 1775. Eliab Harvey died in November 1769 and was buried at Hempstead.

10. Edward Harvey (1718–1778)

Edward was the third son of William and Mary Harvey, and was baptised at Chigwell on 17 August 1718. He entered Westminster School in January 1727, at the age of 8, and left in 1735. He was admitted to Lincoln's Inn a year later. Thereafter he pursued a military career and served with the Dragoons becoming Lieutenant-Colonel of the 6th Dragoons in 1754. He was appointed Adjutant-General of the Forces in 1763, and Lieutenant-General in 1772. Harvey served with distinction in the Seven Years War, and was wounded at Wetter and Kloster Kampen.

Having failed, as we have seen, to obtain a seat in Parliament at the General Election of 1761, an opportunity was found for Harvey to stand at the by-election at Gatton, Surrey, in December 1761 and he was successful. He was returned for Harwich in 1768 and 1774, but rarely spoke in the House, and then only on military matters. As Adjutant-General he had considerable influence over military appointments, and Horace Walpole described Harvey as 'the King's confidential tool for the army'.[30] The King ordered that the Governorship of Portsmouth be given to him in 1773 as a reward for his ability and integrity.

Edward had one son, Edward, although the name of the mother is not known, or whether they married. Edward died in March 1778 and was buried at Hempstead.

11. William Harvey (1754–1779)

The heir of William Harvey (d 1763) was his eldest son, a fourth successive William, who was only nine years old when he inherited Rolls in 1763. He lived for only 25 years but in this short time he was elected a Verderer of Waltham Forest in 1771, when he replaced John Conyers I, and Member of Parliament for Essex in 1775.

Harvey's candidature for Parliament had been unanimously approved at a meeting of the county held while he was abroad,[31] and he was returned unopposed. His one recorded vote was with the Administration, but there is no record of his having spoken in the House.

In the Quarter Sessions minutes there is an erased entry recording that in 1776 John Church had been brought to the Sessions from the Barking House of Correction, where he had been committed for cutting and destroying the wood of William Harvey Esq.[32]

He died unmarried at Chigwell on 24 April 1779 and was buried at Hempstead. Of his four brothers, the eldest (Edward) and the youngest (Thomas) had both predeceased him in 1760. The second brother, Stephen, was killed in America at the Battle of Saratoga in 1779, five months after William's death. Stephen would not in any case have inherited Barringtons because William had left his Chigwell estate, which presumably included the manor, to Thomas Grosvenor of Walthamstow to pay £3,500 to Sir Grey Cooper, and after discharge of this debt, to his brother Eliab. The youngest brother, Eliab, therefore succeeded to Rolls.

The family also saw tragedy in the death of one of William and Emma's daughters, Maria (1755–1822) who married George Wilbraham of Cheshire. She was to die in a carriage accident in Hainault Forest,[33] within a stone's throw of Rolls Park.

12. Rolls Park in the eighteenth century

Early in the eighteenth century a long addition was made to the south-east side of the north east-wing and there were later additions on the south and south-west. On the north wall of the Music Room there was a large family group of the Harveys, signed by Sir Godfrey Kneller and dated 1721. (See also Plate 21.)

The dining room and orangery at the west end of the house, and also the rooms over, were added in 1778. William Harvey's neighbour, George Scott, of Woolston Hall, recorded in a note dated 2 May 1778: 'I stand alone in this Parish, as my neighbour Harvey has not yet his house ready for him, and the rest of the parishioners are mere birds of passage, as is commonly the case so near to town.'

The fact of the absence of the Harvey family from their house, and Scott's reference to it, would seem to indicate the progress of works of a more extensive nature than the ordinary painting and whitewashing.[34]

The Music Room (see Plates 20 and 21) was remarkable for the richness of its decorations. Apart from the many portraits of members of the Harvey family on the walls, the ceiling consisted of a single large panel, with a Greek fretted border running all round. Within this large panel was a smaller one, in the centre of which was a design of scroll work with swags of foliage, flowers and fruit. The overmantel was partly executed in wood and partly in modelled plaster, and consisted of an elaborately moulded broken classic pediment, supported by Ionic columns. The mantel itself was made of Parian marble.[35]

The stable buildings (Plate 18) included a weathercock that bore the initials and date 'WH 1700', and a lead cistern dated 1751.

13. Admiral Sir Eliab Harvey (1758–1830)

Eliab, born on 5 December and baptised at Chigwell on 26 December 1758, was to become the most famous of all the Harveys who lived at Rolls. Eliab was only five years old when his father died in 1763, and his uncle Lieutenant-General Edward Harvey acted as his guardian. He attended both Westminster (1768) and Harrow (1770–1775) schools.

Early life

As a younger son and having little expectation, Eliab was enrolled in the Navy in 1771, at the age of 13, when he was nominally entered on the yacht *William and Mary*. There is some confusion as to when he first joined a ship, as the school lists at Harrow show him still as a pupil until 1775. He served on the frigate *Orpheus* and subsequently the *Lynx* in which he proceeded to the West Indies, and later, during the American War of Independence, he served in North American waters on the *Mermaid*, the

Eagle and the *Liverpool* before returning to England in October 1778. He was promoted to Lieutenant in the *Resolution* in February 1779 but did not join the ship. On his brother's death later in the year, he returned to England and unexpectedly inherited a substantial fortune.

In 1780, he became Member of Parliament for Maldon, when he was returned unopposed at a by-election and at the General Election in the same year. He did not stand in the 1784 election. Being only in his early twenties, he seems not to have taken his life very seriously. He is said to have become a man about town and a reckless gambler, having lost £10,000 in an evening. In a letter dated 6 February 1780 from Sir Horace Walpole to Sir Horace Mann the story is told:

> Within this week there has been a cast at hazard at the Cocoa Tree, the difference of which amounted to an hundred and four score thousand pounds. Mr O'Birne, an Irish gamester, had won one hundred thousand pounds of a young Mr Harvey of Chigwell, just started for a midshipman into an estate, by his elder brother's death. O'Birne said, 'You can never pay me'. 'I can', said the youth, 'my estate will sell for the debt'. 'No', said O. 'I will win ten thousand – you shall throw for the odd ninety'. They did, and Harvey won.

Harvey was back at sea in 1781 on the *Dolphin* and in 1782 on the *Fury* and, by 1783, he had advanced to the rank of Captain on the *Otter*.

In 1784 Eliab married Lady Louisa Nugent, daughter of Earl Nugent. It is said that the Earl did not recognise Louisa as his daughter, but even so the marriage must have brought Eliab influential contacts. They had nine children, all except one of whom were baptised at Chigwell. Eliab seems to have lived most of the time at Rolls after his marriage, avoiding at least those naval duties that might take him away from England, until 1790. He continued the family tradition of taking the office of Surveyor of the Highways for Barringtons Lordship until 1789. In November 1785 he was elected a Verderer of Waltham Forest in succession to Sir William Wake.

In 1790 he was given command of the *Hussar* for a few weeks, but in 1792 he was at Rolls and attended three Vestry meetings during that year. Further postings in 1794 took him away but in 1795 he was home again and attended an important Vestry meeting to draw up recommendations for the relief of the poor. In the same year he and his wife appear in the Hair Powder Tax return. At the Easter Vestry he was nominated by the Vicar as his churchwarden and was duly elected. However, in September, the Vestry book records that the Vicar nominated P A Sapte to be his churchwarden 'in the room of Eliab Harvey Esq who is absent in the service of his Country'. He was recorded as being a Steward at the Harrow Dinner in 1799.[36]

Parliamentary career, 1780–1812

Though still a serving officer with the country at war, Harvey turned from gambling to politics at the age of 22. He was returned for Maldon at the by-election in May 1780 on the death of the Hon Richard Savage Nassau, son of the third Earl of Rochford, who had held the seat since 1774. Harvey owed his seat to his family connection (both his father and brother were MPs for Essex) and in return for agreeing with his fellow member at Maldon, John Strutt, to pay two-thirds of the election expenses. Harvey was not opposed and apparently felt it unnecessary to spend much on the election.

At the General Election in September 1780 it was unusually quiet in the country as a whole, expensive contests being very few. John Strutt of Terling Place (MP for Maldon since 1774) and Eliab Harvey were returned unopposed, although Strutt's correspondence refers to the proposed candidature of Lord Waltham of New Hall, Boreham. The freemen of Maldon were duly thanked and suitably rewarded. A joint address of thanks was issued by Strutt and Harvey on 6 September:

We give you our warmest thanks for the honour of your unanimous return of us again to represent you in Parliament. The appearance, so very numerous and so very respectable on our behalf upon the day of election, though no opposition was publicly declared, is a circumstance which we never can forget.

We shall return to Parliament warm and steady supporters of all those Rights and Privileges which belong to you as Englishmen and of that Old Constitutional Government which alone can insure to you the continuance of them.[37]

The combined expenses of Strutt and Harvey at the uncontested election in September 1780 were £850. John White, Strutt's agent, wanted to knock over £24 off the publicans' accounts unless 'Mr Strutt approves of 8s per pound over charged in 60 pounds of Ham and thinks that six hundred and ninety six bottles of wine, ninety-two gallons of Beer, 28 gallons of Punch, besides Brandy, Rum, Gin and old Beer is a fair charge'.[38]

Harvey was happy to pay his fair share of election expenses, writing to Strutt on 10 January 1781:

I concur with you entirely relative to the allowance for the time of the London voters, as we cannot expect their suffrages in future if we do not make good their losses on our account. If you have any occasion for money for this purpose, you may draw on me, and I will pay the Draft at sight. Many thanks for your kind invitation to Terling Place, am sorry that it is not in my power to accept of it at present, as I am engaged in making preparations for a sea voyage, but hope to see you in town first, that we may conclude our business. I shall not go before the meeting of Parliament, but soon after.[39] [Harvey was referring to resuming his naval career.]

He supported Lord North's administration and was considered a Pittite. In Parliament one correspondent reported that 'We never heard of Mr Harvey's abilities in the House as a speaker, he being content to give a silent vote'.[40]

Strutt's correspondence from December 1783 refers to the threatened dissolution of Parliament and the proposed candidature of Lord Waltham; one of Strutt's supporters, Jacob Patisson of Witham, commented unfavourably on Harvey's suitability:

I sincerely trust some sensible Country Gentleman could be thought instead of a young man who appears to concern himself so very little with business as Mr H does ...

I am confident no opposition will be thought of against you, but I am afraid the lovers of contest will throw out objections to Mr H.[41]

Pattison later reported on the favourable impression created on the electorate by Lord Waltham and the reaction against Harvey: 'It is really melancholy consideration that disapprobation of one gentleman should so violently and suddenly induce people to imbrace the first person offered, though equally improper.'[42]

Harvey was in Paris during December, but had returned to England by the third week of January 1784, when Frank Smythies of Colchester reports on an interview with him:

At length I have seen Mr Harvey who seems wavering and says he shall be determined by what you advise him. He mentioned that he understood you had been prepared to put your son [Holden] in nomination with you. I told him that I knew you had [heard the rumours], but that you would not hear of it. I told him that the Freemen in my neighbourhood were rather disgusted than otherwise at his never having taken any notice of them tho' they had returned him twice without opposition.[43]

Smythies suggested that Harvey would do better to stand for Colchester, while White mentioned the possibility of Harwich, a Treasury borough. Harvey's candidature was not mentioned again, although he did not finally confirm his intention not to stand until a week before the Election.

Harvey resumed his interrupted political career in 1802 when he was returned unopposed as one of the two county members with the Whig, Colonel John Bullock, as the other. Since 1774 it had been customary for each party to take one county seat, thus saving the cost of a contested election. To quote a letter to the Essex freeholders published by Montagu Burgoyne in 1807:

At the General Election, in 1802, Mr Bramston withdrew, and was succeeded by the present Member, Admiral Harvey, of the same [Tory] political principles, these having been ascertained when he represented the Borough of Maldon. At this Election, in 1802, the coalition of the two parties was, if possible, more evident than ever.

Burgoyne was amongst those expressing dissatisfaction at the compromise: 'on the day of nomination I called on the freeholders to vindicate their Rights, and put an end to this unnatural coalition. I assured them that I should be more proud of being instrumental in the Recovery of their Rights, than of being the object of their choice'.

Having failed to persuade any other candidates to stand, Burgoyne said that he

permitted myself to be proposed and though on the show of hands, the Sheriff declared that the majority was in favour of the present members, yet the very great appearance of Freeholders in my favour fully convinced me that my principles were approved of, and that, if I had persevered, my prospect of success would have been favourable, not withstanding that the united strength of the two Parties was leagued against me: but having declared I would abide by the show of hands, I felt myself bound in honour to be governed by it.

Harvey was again returned unopposed with Bullock in 1806, in the afterglow of Trafalgar. Admiral Harvey's services were enthusiastically recalled – his supporters dined at the Black Boy, Chelmsford – the sign exhibited 'Harvey and the Navy of Old England' – showing the Admiral in *Temeraire* engaging two ships of equal force and compelling them to surrender.

Harvey does not seem to have taken part in the by-election of 1810 caused by the death of the veteran Whig, John Bullock. John Archer Houblon of Hallingbury challenged for the Tories the seat which should have gone to the Whig party under the terms of the compromise. He was opposed unsuccessfully by Burgoyne, who had married the daughter of Eliab Harvey, KC, MP, of Claybury (uncle of Admiral Harvey).

At the General Election of 1812, a full-scale contest appeared likely with Harvey and Houblon for the Tories and Charles Western and Burgoyne as Whigs, although the former refused to run in harness with the radical politician. Over a week before the start of the election on 12 October, Harvey announced that 'circumstances of a private nature, combined with the danger of involving myself in expense without limit, induce me to relinquish the important trust you placed in my hands ten years ago'. Harvey wished to give up 'that wrangling House of Commons' but to do so without loss of character: 'I am complained of for not visiting the different towns, but I am idle and like my farm better than the blackguard canvass of low and interested freeholders.'[44]

Burgoyne suggested in his election address that Harvey's withdrawal was evidence of an understanding between Houblon and Western to keep him out: 'The resignation of Admiral Harvey has partly fulfilled my prediction concerning the strength of the Whig interest in this County. Enable me to resist a detestable compromise and you will hear no more of this odious system of modern politics.' On nomination day, Harvey made a savage attack on Burgoyne, accusing him of securing from the government sinecure positions worth £4,000 a year.

Burgoyne never had a chance, and day by day the votes piled up against him. At the end of the seventh day of the election the position was:

Houblon	1417
Western	1251
Burgoyne	339

Burgoyne decided to withdraw, and the successful candidates were carried through the streets of Chelmsford in triumph.

Naval career and Trafalgar Campaign

In 1793, at the outbreak of the French Revolutionary War, Harvey was appointed to the *Santa Margarita* frigate and served under Sir John Jervis at the reduction of Martinique from March to April 1794. (Jervis went on to become Lord St Vincent, another eccentric and cranky old admiral, who lived at Rochetts, South Weald, Essex.[45]) In 1796 Harvey had command of the *Valiant* (74 guns) in the West Indies under Hyde Parker, but he returned to England in 1797 due to ill health. In May he was one of the successful opponents of the Whig petition calling for the dismissal of Pitt's government, which was already facing military defeat, a financial crisis and a naval mutiny. A meeting at Chelmsford broke up in disorder – Western, Honywood and the other Whig speakers being dragged away on the wagon on which they were speaking in front of the Shire Hall.

In March 1798 the government decided to raise a force of Sea Fencibles, recruited from the waterside population to reinforce naval personnel in case of enemy invasion. On 24 March, the *Chelmsford Chronicle* understood that 'Captain Eliab Harvey of Chigwell, is appointed by the Lords Commissioners of the Admiralty to the command of this coast from Leigh to Harwich and is now actively employed in this service'. Conditions of enrolment issued by Harvey include service confined to 'their own coast, except in the event of enemy landing', protection from impressment, watching beaches 'wherever the wind and weather shall be favourable for the enemy to attempt a landing', embarkation 'on board any gun-boat, or other armed vessel for the protection of merchant vessels, when any armed vessel of the enemy shall be in sight'.

By 1799 Harvey was again at sea, commanding the *Triumph* (also 74 guns) in the Channel.

In November 1803 Eliab Harvey was appointed captain of the *Temeraire*, a ship of of 98 guns. After serving in the blockade off Brest and in the Bay of Biscay his ship became part of the Fleet off Cadiz in 1805. By August of that year the French Admiral Villeneuve was threatening not only England's shores, but the merchant fleets by which in the last resort she lived. Nelson's combination of Mediterranean and Channel fleet provided the opportunity to counter attack.

On 19 October, two days before the Battle of Trafalgar, Villeneuve left Cadiz with 33 French and Spanish ships. Nelson planned the attack to be made in two main columns: Collingwood's Lee column to attack the enemy's rear, and Nelson's Weather column to steer towards the centre aiming at a point two miles ahead of the enemy's leading ship.

At 11.35am on 21 October Nelson hoisted his famous signal on the *Victory:* 'England expects that every man will do his duty'. Nelson, on Blackwood's suggestion, ordered *Temeraire* and *Leviathan* to pass *Victory*, but when Harvey was on the point of overtaking *Victory*, Nelson signalled him astern by flag, one account says by hailing in person: 'I'll thank you, Captain Harvey, to keep in your proper station, which is astern of the *Victory*.' At noon the *Royal Sovereign* started firing and at 25 minutes after noon the *Victory* opened fire on the French *Redoutable* and the *Temeraire* followed suit against the Spanish *Santissima Trinidad*. Soon the *Temeraire* had the top of her mizzen mast shot away by the *Redoutable*.

The log of the *Temeraire* for 21 October includes the entry: 'At 25 minutes past noon the *Victory* opened her fire. Immediately put our helm aport to steer clear of the *Victory*, and opened our fire against the *Santissima Trinidad* and two ships ahead of her, when the action became general.'

In a letter to his wife, written on 23 October 1805, Harvey wrote:

For nearly two hours we were so nearly engaged that I can give you no other account of this part of this most glorious day's work than what immediately concerned the *Victory* or myself. We were engaged with the *Santissima Trinidad* and other ships for perhaps 20 minutes or more, when for a minute or two I ceased fire, fearing I might from the thickness of the smoke be firing into the *Victory*, but I soon saw the *Victory* close on board a French ship of two decks, and having the Ship [*Temeraire*] under command, notwithstanding we had suffered much in our masts, and sails, etc, I placed the ship so as to give the *Redoutable* a most severe dressing by raking her fore and aft, however, the *Victory* fell back on board of her and she struck. Soon after they tried to board the *Temeraire* so that the Frenchman was exactly between the two Ships being upon my Larboard side. Some time previous to this, finding I could do nothing further with the Ship, I had commenced upon another ship [*Fougeux*] with my Larboard guns and very soon put her into so disabled a state, that we fell on board her also, and she struck. I sent Lieutenant Kennedy, my first, with a party of men to secure this prize, and finding the *Victory* had got clear from *Redoutable*, I sent my second Lieutenant to secure her and ordered both ships to be securely lashed to the *Temeraire*.[46]

The fire of the *Temeraire* was decisive in removing all danger to *Victory* from *Redoutable*. The latter's captain wrote that 'it is impossible to describe the carnage produced by the murderous broadside of this ship. More than 200 of our brave men were killed or wounded by it. All our own guns were either smashed or dismounted by broadsides of *Victory* and *Temeraire*.' The mainmast of *Redoutable* fell on *Temeraire* whose two topmasts then fell on *Redoutable*. *Fougeux* fell on board *Temeraire* on her starboard side, 'so that four ships of the line were rubbing sides in the heat of the fight, with their heads all lying the same way, as if moored in harbour', according to an officer on the *Victory*.

A panorama by W L Wyllie (1851–1931), in the Royal Naval Museum at Portsmouth, shows how *Victory* and *Redoutable* were held together by entanglement in the rigging, but the French were unable to board *Victory* as a result of the starboard carronade and broadside from *Temeraire*, whose rigging became entangled with *Redoutable's* bowsprit.

The *Annual Register* in describing the battle said:

Where all were equally brave, it is difficult to point out individual merit in this well-fought day, but the circumstance of the *Temeraire*, Captain Harvey, who nobly seconded Lord Nelson, having been boarded by a French line of battleship on one side, and a Spanish[47] on the other, and compelling both, after a vigorous contest, to strike her, is too remarkable, and too much to the credit of that gallant officer and his crew, not to merit particular mention.[48]

In a letter to her son-in-law, William Lloyd, Lady Louisa expressed her hope that her daughter, Louisa, would collect in a book all that she had written to her about the *Temeraire's* part at Trafalgar, as she did not have the time herself. In the letter to William Lloyd she recounts that:

The *Redoutable* fell on Board *Temeraire* by her Main Mast falling on *Temeraire's* Poop, together with three beautiful little brass carronades with which the Admiral means to commemorate this event yearly in May on the Mount at Chigwell, by firing them off. The *Redoutable* while securely lashed to *Temeraire* threw combustible matter down one of the Hatchways, while the men were handing up Powder which set fire to them, occasioning an explosion which killed two men. Providentially the fire was put out or else the three ships [*Temeraire, Redoutable* and *Fougeux*] must have blown up. *Temeraire* was nearly if not actually on fire three times.[49]

The *Temeraire's* log records that she ceased firing at 4.30pm, and the Battle of Trafalgar was over less than an hour later. The battered British fleet next day made its way to Gibraltar but for two days gales lashed the limping ships. In a letter to his wife, Harvey wrote:

> The state of the *Temeraire* is so bad, that we have been in constant apprehension of our lives, every sail and yard having been destroyed, and nothing but the lower masts left standing, the rudder-head almost shot off and is since quite gone, and lower masts all shot through and through in many places.

The *Temeraire*, however, managed to come through safely and on 30 October was taken in tow to Gibraltar by the *Defiance*, where she arrived on 2 November, 12 days after Trafalgar. At Gibraltar the *Temeraire* was patched up and refitted sufficiently to enable her to proceed to England under sail.

Admiral Collingwood specially mentioned *Temeraire* in his Trafalgar despatch and wrote to Harvey:

> I congratulate you most sincerely on the victory His Majesty's Fleet has obtained over the Enemy, and on the Noble and distinguished part the *Temeraire* took in the Battle; nothing could be finer; I have not words in which I can sufficiently express my admiration of it.
>
> I hope to hear you are unhurt; and pray send me your report of killed and wounded with the officers names who fell in the action; and the state of your own ship, whether you can get her in a condition to meet Gravina should he again attempt anything.

Some of Harvey's fellow commanders were, however, not so enthusiastic. Captain Codrington said: 'There will always be some whose vanity leads them to paint their conduct in too warm a tint, and to sound their trumpets without regard to concord or harmony, but above all I have ever heard is Harvey . . . He is become the greatest bore I ever met with.' Captain Freemantle: 'Eliab Harvey goes with the next five ships, his head is turned, never having been in action before he thinks every ship was subdued by him, and he wears us all to death with his incessant jargon.'[50]

Harvey was promoted Rear Admiral on 9 November 1805. In a letter dated 2 December 1805, Lady Louisa Harvey recorded that, at a county meeting held at Chelmsford on 29 November, before the return of the *Temeraire*, 'all were unanimous in speaking in the highest manner of him. Lord Braybrook began in his praise, Lord St Vincent seconded him, and Mr Burgoyne even proposed that a subscription should be raised for the *Temeraire* crew. However, that was not carried.'[51] Harvey received the thanks of Parliament, and more substantial rewards in the shape of a gold medal and sword of honour.

Harvey returned to Portsmouth with the *Temeraire* at the beginning of December, nearly six weeks after Trafalgar. Forty-seven of the crew had been killed in the battle and 31 badly injured. Later, on 7 December, Lady Louisa wrote enthusiastically that 'all the *Temeraire's* men look so happy, so proud, when the weather is fine, boats go in quantity to row round her, and a draftsman went off today to take her picture'.[52]

The Harveys were in London by 9 December and plans were made for a reception by the Yeomanry at Chigwell. Some sailors from the *Temeraire* were also in London and Lady Louisa had been told that 'they get hats full of silver on the exchange'. The local gentry at Chigwell organised a subscription dinner in his honour at the King's Head, on 9 November 1805, the tickets for which were priced at the then prodigious sum of five guineas, and an annual 'Trafalgar Celebration Dinner' was held at the same place for many years after. Harvey was one of the pall-bearers at Lord Nelson's funeral.

Harvey was longing to see his eldest daughter and first grandchild. In a letter to Louisa Lloyd on 7 December 1805 he wrote:

I do hope that you will have some compassion and come to visit a poor half pay Rear Admiral who has been bustling about in the Busy World until he has become quite anxious to enjoy for a short time the comforts of Domestic Society, and which he fears the present state of Europe will not admit of his doing for any length of time.[53]

The Temeraire

The first ship to be named *Temeraire* (the best translation of the name is 'Reckless' or 'Daring') was built for Louis XIV in 1668. The ship was one of the French squadron which, at the opening of the third Dutch War in 1672, fought as an ally of England. Twenty years later she fought as an enemy at Cape Barfleur. Three other French *Temeraires* followed, the last of these being a 74-gun ship built in 1748. This ship was captured by Admiral Boscawen in his battle with Admiral de la Clue off Lagos in August 1759. She served in the British Navy for some years and, after being utilised as a floating battery at Plymouth during the American War, was finally sold out of service in 1784.

In 1788 the Lords Commissioners of the Admiralty ordered four 98-gun ships of war to be built. These were to be named the *Temeraire*, *Dreadnought*, *Neptune* and *Ocean*. The *Temeraire* was an Essex ship, built – nine-tenths of her – of oak cut in Hainault Forest[54] and sent across to Chatham dockyard, where the *Temeraire's* keel was laid in July 1793. She was a three-decker, a second-rate, 2,121 tons, 'a ninety-eight' in the navy parlance of the time, a ship carrying 98 guns, with her guns, ranging from 12 to 32 pounders, dispersed over the gun, middle and quarter decks, and the forecastle. She was launched on 11 September 1798, and was commissioned in March 1799, her first captain being Peter Puget.[55]

Temeraire's first assignment was to the blockade of the Channel ports, sometimes off Brest, at others in the Bay of Biscay. In October 1801 an armistice was agreed and the preliminaries of peace were signed. After the dull, weary, eventless months of the blockade, the fleet looked forward to returning to England. Many of the men had not seen home or family for a number of years. However, while lying off Bantry Bay, Admiral George Campbell's squadron, which included the *Temeraire*, heard the news that they were not to sail for England and home, but for the West Indies. On 7 December 1801 a number of the crew of the *Temeraire* mutinied, and offered violence to their Admiral and officers. Retribution was swift with eleven of the *Temeraire's* men hanged at the yard-arm, following a court-martial held at Portsmouth in January 1802, and the crew were paid off.

Captain Eliab Harvey was appointed to commission the *Temeraire* with a new crew at Plymouth, in November 1803, six months after the outbreak of the war with Napoleon. Harvey manned his ship to a large extent with Liverpool men, and sailed from Cawsand Bay on 11 March 1804 to join Admiral Cornwallis off Brest.

After Trafalgar, the battered *Temeraire* was partly refitted at Gibraltar. She returned to Spithead on 5 December 1805 and six months later was paid off for refit and repair in Portsmouth dockyard. For six years after Trafalgar, the *Temeraire* continued on active service until she was finally paid off at Portsmouth on 20 March 1812. From that time, she was employed on various routine duties, her last being Guardship at Sheerness. The last guns ever fired by the *Temeraire* were for the Royal Salute in honour of Queen Victoria's coronation.

How Turner came to paint his *'Fighting Temeraire'* is a story in itself. The famous picture came into being by the merest accident; as the outcome of a happy chance, the result of a casual meeting with the old ship at a water-picnic on the Thames one autumn evening in 1838. Turner, with some friends, was boating off Greenwich marshes in Blackwall Reach when the old ship passed them, coming up the river from Sheerness to meet her destined end off Rotherhithe, where the ship-breaker Beatson's men were waiting for her. She had been sold out of the service some days before for £5,530, barely the market value of the copper bolts that held her timbers together. The grand old man-of-war looked forlorn. Her sails stripped from the yards, her tiers of ports without guns and closed down, her hull with its last coat of dockyard drab all rusty-looking and weather-stained. Two tugs had the ship in tow, not one as Turner has painted. '*The Fighting* Temeraire *tugged to her last berth to be broken up*', was the title Turner gave his picture when he sent it in to the Royal Academy Exhibition of 1839. Lady Louisa Harvey is said to have declined Turner's offer of his painting of the ship on the grounds that £200 was too much for a painting by a living artist.

A view by Schetky shows *Temeraire* off Spithead, and, in 1867, a painting was exhibited of her entering Portsmouth harbour.[56]

The Maritime Museum at Greenwich has a small table from Harvey's cabin, and a barometer made from the *Temeraire's* timbers. In the church of St Mary's, Rotherhithe, there are two Bishop's chairs and, in the Epiphany Chapel, a Communion Table, made of oak from the *Temeraire*.[57]

The Royal Navy later had a third *Temeraire,* this time a battleship built at Chatham in 1876, and a fourth and last *Temeraire,* a battleship of 18,600 tons, was built at Devonport in 1907 and sold for breaking up in 1921.[58]

Court-martial

Harvey was promoted to the rank of Rear Admiral of the Blue in 1806, and hoisted his flag in the *Tonnant,* in which he joined the Channel Fleet under Lord St Vincent, by whom he was detached with a separate squadron off the Spanish coast. When Lord St Vincent retired, he wrote to Harvey in April 1807:

> I cannot retire from the command of the Channel Fleet, without expressing the high sense I entertain of the ability, zeal, and perseverance displayed by you, in the command of a detached squadron, during an unexampled long cruise off the north coast of Spain; and of assuring you of the esteem and regard with which I have the honour to be, &c. &c.[59]

Harvey was at home in the autumn of 1807 when he made an inspection of an enclosure in the Forest, and reported his view to the Court of Attachments. However, his active naval career was only to last for another three years.

When on duty with the Channel Fleet in 1809, Harvey was infuriated by the fact that he was not put in command of the attack on the Basque Roads, Lord Cochrane being preferred to him. His wife's letters later pictured him as irascible and hot-tempered, and it may well be imagined that when he impetuously expressed his anger and disgust at being passed over, on the quarter deck of his flagship before his junior officers, he did not mince his words. A court-martial was inevitable. The court met on 21 May 1809 with

Admiral Sir Roger Curtis acting as President, supported by eight admirals and four captains. Harvey had retained Serjeant Best to defend him at a fee of 300 guineas. A good description of the proceedings appeared in the *Gentleman's Magazine*:

Portsmouth: The Court Martial assembled on board the *Gladiator* for the trial of Rear-Admiral Harvey, on charges which impute disrespect to his superior officer, Admiral Lord Gambier, Commander in Chief of the Channel Fleet, and which charges are comprised in two letters addressed to the Secretary of the Admiralty. The first letter stated that when he (Lord Gambier) had informed Rear-Admiral Harvey that the Admiralty had ordered Lord Cochrane to be employed in attempting to destroy the enemy fleet in Basque Roads, the Rear-Admiral declared in the most violent disrespectful manner, and desired Lord Gambier to consider it as official communication, that, if he was passed by, and Lord Cochrane, or any junior officer, appointed in preference, he should immediately desire to strike his flag, and resign his commission. In the progress of the conversation, the Rear-Admiral complained of his having been neglected both by Lord Gambier and other Members of former Boards of Admiralty; and declared, that he had differed with him with respect to his conduct in the command of his fleet, and that he would impeach him for misconduct and bad management.

The second letter requested a Court Martial to be held upon Rear-Admiral Harvey. Lord Gambier, Sir H B Neale, Captains Beresford and Bowen, and Lord Cochrane, were severally examined in support of the charges. The latter admitted that Admiral Harvey has said that he was no canting Methodist, no hypocrite, nor no psalm-singer; but it was evidently unpremeditated, and arose from the warmth of his feelings at the moment.

At half past nine on Tuesday the Court re-assembled, when the Rear-Admiral Harvey shortly stated his intention not to trouble the Court with calling any witnesses; but delivered in a paper which he desired to be read. This request was complied with. In the paper the Rear-Admiral observed, that the charges had not been sustained; that he could not justify one part of his conduct; for which he offered an apology to the Court; that, for the offence he had given to Lord Gambier, he had already offered an apology satisfactory to his feelings; that his remarks had been made to officers of rank only, and at a time when he was greatly irritated, in consequence of his offer of attacking the French fleet having been passed over without any acknowledgement of its having been made; in fine, that excess of zeal, and impatience of restraint, where an opportunity of enterprise presents itself, although faults, are such as the most eminent Naval Commanders have not been free from; and the effects of these are all that can found blameable in his conduct.

To the paper were appended two letters; one from Adm. Collingwood, the other from Earl St Vincent, both acknowledging, in high terms, the meritorious services of Rear Adm. Harvey. After a short deliberation, the Deputy Judge Advocate declared, that the Court were of opinion that the charge of using insulting language to Lord Gambier, as well as speaking disrespectfully of him to several officers had been proved; and adjudged Rear-Admiral Harvey to be dismissed his Majesty's service.[60]

The verdict, although inevitable, was undoubtedly unpopular with the British public, and there were widespread misgivings concerning the fairness

Plate 1
Eliab Harvey (1589–1661)

Plate 2
Mary Harvey (1607–1673)

Plate 3
Sir Eliab Harvey (1635–1699)

Plate 4
Lady Dorothy Harvey (1638–1725)

Plate 5
William Harvey (1663–1731)

Plate 6
Dorothy Harvey (1688–1711)

Plate 7
William Harvey (1714–1763)

Plate 8
Emma Harvey (1732–1767)

Plate 9
Edward Harvey (1718–1778)

Plate 10
Stephen Harvey (1757–1779)

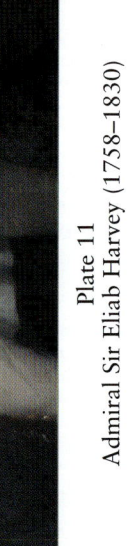

Plate 12
Admiral Sir Eliab Harvey:
Hatchment in St Andrew's Church, Hempstead

Plate 11
Admiral Sir Eliab Harvey (1758–1830)

Plate 13
Battle of Trafalgar: Captain Harvey clearing the deck of the French and Spanish

Plate 14
Battle of Trafalgar: Situation of the *Temeraire* at 3 pm, 21 October 1805

Plate 15
Temeraire entering Portsmouth Harbour, December 1805

Plate 16
The North West Front, Rolls Park

Plate 17
The Garden Front, Rolls Park

Plate 18
The Stables, Rolls Park

Plate 19
The Grand Staircase, Rolls Park

Plate 20
The Music Room, Rolls Park, with the earliest group of portraits

Plate 21
The Music Room, Rolls Park, with a family group by Sir Godfrey Kneller

of the court-martial, and it was no doubt public opinion that led to the Admiralty reinstating Harvey as Rear Admiral of the Red in March 1810,[61] 'in consideration of his long and meritorious services', and at the same time he was presented to the King.[62] Later in the year he was promoted to Vice-Admiral of the Blue, and in August 1819 to a full Admiral. However, he never carried out any naval duties after his court-martial.

Country squire and parliamentarian

Eliab now settled down to live the life of country squire and county parliamentarian. In 1809 he was a Steward at the Annual Dinner of the True Blue Club at Colchester,[63] and in 1810 he served on the grand jury at the Essex Lenten Assizes.[64] As we have seen Harvey withdrew his candidature a week before the General Election in October 1812. Within a month he received the news of the death of his eldest son, Captain Edward Harvey, at the siege of Burgos, while serving with the Coldstream Guards.

In 1816, with a sudden agricultural depression, Eliab set an example by reducing his rents by 10 shillings an acre. Having been knighted in 1815, he no doubt felt that he was important enough to have influence with his neighbours. However, the memory of his sad dismissal from the Navy made Eliab bitter and irascible. His wife, writing to her eldest daughter, Louisa Lloyd, in 1818, noted the change in his temperament. 'We are all in a bad way at Chigwell', she wrote on one occasion, 'Never was anything equal to him, the whole village and neighbourhood are talking of him'. Later in the year she lamented:

> I am convinced that he [Sir Eliab] is insane. Two nights ago he attacked me and gave Maria a frightful blow to the head; he has also shown his madness at five or six different times by pulling off every one of the young vine shoots, pulling up all the French beans, and breaking off a dozen hyacinths and treading in the roots under his feet.'

In 1788 Harvey had been appointed a Governor of Chigwell School, and remained so for 42 years. In 1818 he became a trustee of the newly formed Ongar Hundred Savings Bank and, in the same year, he presided at a meeting of the Central Committee of the parishes situated within the boundaries of Waltham, Epping and Hainault Forests, held at the London Tavern,[65] formed to deal with the increasing encroachments. In 1819, shortly after he had been promoted to full Admiral, he and his family attended a fete in the grounds of William Sotheby's house at Fairmead.

Harvey spent many thousands of pounds on improving Rolls Park. His wife, Lady Louisa, wrote in July 1820 that 'the house is full of workmen making flues to warm the house. They have taken up all the pavement in every direction in the passages', but in January 1827 she still complained that 'this house is certainly the coldest in England'. A painting of Rolls Park at about this time appeared in J P Neale's, *Views of the Seats of Noblemen and Gentlemen in England, Wales, Scotland and Ireland* (1826).

His attitude to money is a constant theme. In August 1821 Lady Louisa had been told 'the Admiral is losing considerably by not letting his Chigwell Hall Farm, that is managed in such a bad way now it remains in his hands'.[66] Visitors had to be warned about one of the Admiral's economies and the danger of being poisoned

> with the putrid smell which is all over the lower part of the House and in poor Emma's Bed Room, proceeding from the Meat, which actually tastes and smells. The Admiral will not own to it, merely that he may not be at expense . . . the Meat being now in the Cellar, pounds of it is always thrown away, so much for Admiral Stingy with his fine lumps of Money lent out on interest.

This sum totalled £30,000 or £35,000 and probably represented his total capital two years before his death. The letters are full of the Admiral's passion for abusing and dismissing servants including a cook with 35 years' service. Lady Louisa was 'quite enchanted with the new gardener, everything now looks flourishing and clean, before he came everything looking dying and dirty', but the new butler was not such a success,

> never in your life did you see such an old half crazy extraordinary man as the Butler, not the slightest idea of his place; coming out of a warehouse in the India House where he had some department, he had been all these days doing most extraordinary things, the Admiral, however, only being in a rage when ever he saw him until this morning [when] the Old Man did not choose to answer the Admiral's Bell, he therefore sent for the Cart and ordered him in it and sent him off.

In another letter Lady Louisa says she is 'extremely satisfied with the gardener. He is a most honest, sober and a most excellent servant to trust besides being an excellent gardener.'[67]

Harvey's many local interests persuaded him once more to seek election to Parliament. Writing to his daughter Louisa on 10 March 1820, Harvey was confident that: 'On Monday next I shall be chosen Member for the county of Essex without opposition. I am sure that you will rejoice to hear that Houblon has retired.' He was an ardent Tory and a sound, though seemingly inarticulate, Member. In July his long-suffering wife was writing to her daughter Louisa: 'The Admiral is wrapped up in the House of Commons and can give his mind to no one other thing. He has not been to Chigwell these six weeks.'

As might be expected at this stage of his career, one of his main concerns was on behalf of the farming interests. In March 1823 his only surviving son, William, died at Rolls after a short illness, having only just attained his majority. Also in 1823 he presented a petition from Essex to the House of Commons praying for the repeal of the duty on malt, and said that the petition spoke for itself, and then complained of the absence of County Members in important divisions.[68] Sir Eliab was one of the first patrons of the Essex Economic Fire Assurance Association formed in 1824.[69] A year later he was honoured by promotion to GCB.

Early in 1826 Lady Louisa was planning for her eldest daughter to come to Rolls in the hope of preventing the Admiral carting the whole family up to London, as he must be there 'chiefly for his parliament'. Parliament was dissolved in June 1826, Harvey again being returned unopposed at the subsequent election.

In the same year a meeting was held at Chelmsford for considering 'the abolition of Colonial Slavery', and he was deputed by the meeting to present its petition to the House of Commons.[70] Within the next year he showed his intense hostility towards Catholic emancipation, and was so embittered when the Act was passed, that he never again took any interest in his parliamentary duties.

In 1827 an elderly housemaid at Sir Eliab's London house, in Clifford Street, off Bond Street, was charged with having stolen his Trafalgar medal, his decoration of the Order of the Bath, a full dress uniform and various other articles. However, she was discharged, but as only a short report of the case has been found it is not known how strong or weak was the evidence against her.[71]

His wife's letters to her eldest daughter give evidence of Eliab's obstinacy. This was also illustrated by a civil action brought against him at Essex Lenten Assizes in 1829 by Mr Boote, the lay-impropriator (or possessor) of the rectorial tithes of Chigwell, for recovery of tithes of hay and clover on Harvey's lands. It was said that the latter had refused to set out his crops in the proper manner, and a verdict was given for the plaintiff, damages being assessed at £30.[72]

Admiral Sir Eliab Harvey died at Rolls Park in February 1830 and was buried in the Harvey vault at Hempstead – his gothic monument was designed by Humphrey Hopper and is surmounted by his arms and crest with the mottoes *Temeraire* (above) and *Redoutable et Fougeux* (below). The funeral procession wound its way across Essex from Rolls. Family tradition has it that the Essex hounds crossed the procession which was at once halted – the mourners jumped from their carriages and 'view halloed' the hounds on, one of the loudest being William Lloyd the chief mourner![73] An obituary said of Harvey that he,

> as a magistrate was remarkable for a firmness and decision, which some considered as approximating too closely to a rigid dispensation of justice, but in his private friendship he was sincere and constant, and what redounds still more to his praise, he was a kind, liberal and indulgent landlord.[74]

A month later the sale took place at Mr Philip's Great Rooms in New Bond Street of 'Admiral Harvey's Cellar of Choice Wines lying at Rolls Park and his valuable Mathematical Instruments'. The sale included 150 dozen of port, Stainforth's Sherry, old Madeira Hock, and ten flasks of Maraschino; also three telescopes, two compasses and a quadrant.[75]

14. Lady Louisa Harvey

Lady Louisa Harvey continued to live at Rolls after her husband's death. From her many letters it appears that she had little intercourse with the Chigwell gentry for very few references are made to them, although there are passing references to her dealings with local tradesmen. It seems that she regarded her social standing far above that of the Chigwell residents and that her level was rather with the aristocratic and landed classes of the County, including such families as the Conyers of Copped Hall, Epping, and the Burgoynes of Mark Hall, Latton.

Lady Louisa's letters to her eldest daughter, Louisa, born in 1785, are full of the doings of her other five daughters and only surviving son, William. A portrait by Lawrence shows her with Louisa and her son Edward. The letters also complain about her health, but she survived her aggravating husband and died at Skreens, the home of her daughter Eliza Bramston, at the age of 84.

Letters also reveal the relationship with Admiral Harvey in the last decades of his life, particularly after William's death in 1823. A trip to Paris in the following year drove Lady Louisa almost to despair. In a letter, dated 3 May, she wrote:

> Your Father's temper is really so bad that I am annoyed to death and worried out of my life with him, it all falls on me as he is mighty civil and smiling to them [his four unmarried daughters]. I get out of all patience, my health and spirits are not equal to it, after all I have gone through lately [including her daughter Georgiana's premature confinement] and shall give the thing quite up and leave him and them to live together. The Admiral has not (except of abuse God knows why) said three words to me since his arrival here [four weeks ago].[76]

Three or four years later the servant problem was exacerbated by the Admiral's interference and the atmosphere of armed neutrality at Rolls:

> I am all in the misery about new servants and it is a real misery for the Admiral's temper is so outrageous to me as well as to them that it all takes its chance, as I cannot speak to him on the subject, as he never utters to me but abuse, I therefore seldom go down but to dinner unless any one comes, and at dinner it is horrid to hear him scold the servants, and I expect it myself. His eyes staring out of his head and a settled furious cross countenance ready to fly at and eat up everyone.[77]

In 1832, soon after she was widowed, Lady Louisa had an unpleasant experience as a result of dismissing her butler, William Hall, 'in consequence of some recent irregularities'; he thereupon shot himself in his pantry at Rolls just as his mistress was about to enter her coach.[78] From her letters we learn that she had continuously had difficulties with servants; if she employed them, her husband soon dismissed them, while he engaged those she found quite unsuitable.

15. Eliab and Louisa Harvey's family

It was thought that Sir Eliab would leave his estate divided among his five surviving daughters, but when his will was read, it was found that he had left the bulk of his property, including Barringtons, to his eldest daughter, Louisa, who had married William Lloyd of Aston Hall in Shropshire. Mr Lloyd and his wife appear in the court rolls as joint lords until his death in 1843 after which his widow acted as sole lord until she died in 1866. However, it is certainly doubtful if they ever lived at Rolls.

Certainly no father could have written more tenderly to his first born than did Captain Harvey on the *Temeraire* to his nineteen-year-old daughter on the eve of her engagement in July 1804:

> I am sure you have reflected and reflected most seriously upon the prospect before you. If we had not understood each other it would have been useless for me to attempt to give you advice; every word which I have heard concerning Mr Lloyd convinces me you have felt the conversations we have had on this important subject and that your sound judgement has taught you to act upon the principles which I strove to fix in your mind. That I should have a most anxious wish to be with you and to have conversed and consulted with you at an earlier stage of your Attachment, you will not be surprised, but if your heart as well as your judgement accord upon this important occasion, I shall have nothing to regret (I can imagine no one event in life more interesting to me than seeing my Dearest Louisa comfortably placed for life with the man of her own choice . . .)
>
> [After the wedding in October 1804:] Had I been at Home I might have done worse but could not have done better so may God bless you as you deserve to be happy.

Louisa Lloyd's portrait was painted by Sir George Hayter. Rolls came to Louisa when the estates were divided by lot on the Admiral's death, but her father had not always been sympathetic to requests for financial help during his lifetime – an appeal in 1825, the year of Maria's wedding to the Rev William Tower, received a curt reply: 'you must know my expenses have been and must be very great this year.'

Her mother advised her to return to the attack in October 1828 when the Admiral was in a surprisingly good mood: 'I wish to goodness you would not let this quiet tone pass over without making an attempt at the Money Bag . . . if you will allude to his generosity to your married sisters I think you may succeed.'

Eliab and Louisa's eldest son, William, died in 1794 at the age of eight years. Edward became a captain in the Coldstream Guards, but at the age of 22, on 18 October 1812, 'he fell honourably in the lines of Burgos' in Wellington's futile and abortive siege.

A second William, who was born in December 1801, died after a short illness in March 1823. He was educated at Brasenose College, Oxford, but appears to have suffered from poor health. William caught a cough going up to London from Rolls in cold weather. The family doctor, Dr Holland slept at Rolls every night. Lady Louisa, writing to her eldest daughter on 3 March 1823, comments that

he [William] keeps his bed, is lifted out and in, the great misery is the great accumulation of phlegm on his chest which he has not power to throw up, and they dare not give an emetic nor dare they bleed, his constitution being too feeble. . . . He has had a large blister on [his chest]. He now chiefly is to live on Asses milk but is ordered to have nourishment (no solids) every three hours regularly. Maria and Eliza sit up alternately in his room at night, his servant is in the Dressing Room.[79]

The Admiral added a postscript to his wife's letter: 'in my opinion I cannot think my dear William any better than she has stated him to be.'[80]

After William's death, Lady Louisa begged her daughter Louisa to 'come to this House of Misery'[81]; and Georgiana's husband, John Drummond wrote, on 4 March, to William Lloyd that 'the state of this family which is truly distressing though they bear up with more firmness than I could have expected and last night was a dreadful night but they have slept towards morning'.[82]

The second eldest daughter, Emma, was born in 1787 and did not marry until a few days before her father's death; her husband was Colonel William Cornwallis Eustace of Sampford, Essex, who took her as his third wife. Maria, born in 1791, married in 1825, the Rev William Tower, a member of the South Weald family; he was a man of little wealth and the match was not regarded by her mother with enthusiasm. Georgiana, born in 1796, married in 1816 John Drummond, a member of a wealthy banking family. Still unmarried when their father died were the two youngest daughters. Elizabeth, born in 1798, who married, five months later, Thomas William Bramston of Skreens in Roxwell, for many years Member of Parliament for Essex. Isabella Mary, born in 1806, married George Robert Cecil Fane in 1835 and died three years later. All the daughters were married at St George's, Hanover Square, except Emma, who was married at Loughton. It is perhaps interesting to note that the respective ages at marriage were 17, 42, 36, 20, 32, and 28, which suggests it was no easy task for Lady Louisa to make suitable marriages for such a large family of girls.

16. Rolls Park in the nineteenth and early twentieth centuries

After Lady Louisa Harvey's death in 1841, Rolls Park was mainly occupied by tenants. The Census return of 1851 shows Edward Charrington, aged 39, with his wife Georgiana, their five small children, eight indoor servants, with a gardener and a groom living in the outhouses with their families. A year later, on the death of his elder brother, Mr Charrington and his family moved to the family's ancestral seat of Bures Manor, Surrey, and Rolls was taken by Sir William Abraham Chatterton, 2nd baronet, who lived there with his wife until his death in 1855. His wife, Lady Henrietta Georgiana Marcia Lascelles Chatterton, was an authoress of some note.

In 1862 a Mrs Fletcher was in occupation, and in 1874 J H Crossman. He was followed by Edward Ash Ball who lived at Rolls with his wife, Elizabeth, until their deaths in 1884 and 1878, respectively. William Walter Radford came to Rolls about 1890; he died aged 42 in 1897 and was buried at Chigwell. His wife remained at Rolls until the end of the century. After she left, Vivian Hugh Smith, later Lord Bicester, took up residence with his wife, Lady Sybil, daughter of the 6th Earl of Antrim. He was well known in banking spheres, his father having been Governor of the Bank of England. They were well known locally and lived at Rolls until shortly before the First World War.

On Louisa Lloyd's death in 1866, her only surviving son, Richard Thomas Lloyd, inherited the manor of Barringtons. He died in 1898 when the manor passed to his eldest son, then Brigadier-General, but later Lieutenant-General, Sir Francis Lloyd, GCVO, KCB, DSO. In 1913 Sir

Francis Lloyd was appointed as GOC, London District, and it was natural that he should come to live at Rolls rather than at his other property in Shropshire. He married Miss Mary Gunnis, but they had no children. Sir Francis was a governor of Chigwell School from 1923–1926 and was Chairman during part of this period.

On the death of Sir Francis in 1926, the manor passed to Sir Francis's brother, the Rev Rossendale Lloyd, rector of Selattyn in Shropshire. He soon after sold the manorial rights, but not the freehold of the estate, to Mr Philip Savill, a member of a well-known Chigwell family. In 1839 the estate in Chigwell had consisted of about 420 acres.[83] With the Rev Rossendale Lloyd, living in Shropshire, Rolls became empty. It was, however, later let for a few years to A C M Spearman.

An inventory of the contents of Rolls Park taken in 1932 indicates that there were at least 15 bedrooms.

17. Life at Rolls Park in the 1920–1930s

In 1978 a former servant at Rolls Park, Mrs Hems, was interviewed about her time there when Lady Mary Lloyd, widow of Sir Francis Lloyd, was still living in the house. A transcript of the recording of the interview was subsequently published in the December 1978 Newsletter of the Chigwell Local History Society.[84] It gives a fascinating insight into life in a bygone age:

It was in April 1929 when I went to Rolls Park. I'd always lived in London and I thought how lovely it seemed. I sat in the servants' hall and the cook – Miss Carrie Roberts – gave me tea. I heard the birds singing. I was about 17 then and a housemaid. I thought Rolls Park was a wonderful house It had an atmosphere as though all the people who lived there had led happy lives and had left something of themselves.

We were a happy band of workers there. There was Mr Humphrey, the butler, Miss Roberts, the cook, and Miss Woodward who was Lady Lloyd's personal maid. We also had a kitchen maid. They used to come from Barnardo's homes, stay for a time and then be replaced by another girl. We had a chauffeur who used to do odd jobs in the house as well.

We used to get up at half-past six in the morning. It was hard in the winter because although we had central heating there were great fires which were iron and brass so that I had blackleading to do and brass to clean. My hands were always chapped and grimed with dirt, although I always wore gloves.

Each morning I went round the house and undid all the big wooden shutters which folded right back. There was such a clatter because they had big iron bars on them but nobody complained. I had the Dining Room, the Morning Room, the Library, the Music Room and the big hall to do before I had my breakfast, and of course, we didn't have vacuum cleaners. I polished the floor with a mixture I made up myself by breaking up pieces of beeswax and shaking them in a jar of turpentine until they dissolved. The floor absorbed it quickly and it took a lot of rubbing off but it looked lovely when it was finished.

I had a little dog – Lady Lloyd's Pekinese. I used to take it out for a walk and then we'd have our breakfast. Then I would go upstairs to the bedrooms. Although they were not being used they had to be freshened and dusted every day and an awful lot of brass to clean.

I thoroughly enjoyed it all. I was left to do it as I liked and the ornaments and pictures were so beautiful that it was a joy to handle them. Nearly all of them had a history and were mementoes of Sir Francis Lloyd's military service. I remember a silver cigarette case, all open work and pieces of stained glass from Ypres Cathedral from the war when it was bombed. There was a big alabaster statue on a base in a glass case and the case was bound with lead from the first Zeppelin shot down in England. There were also flags of the different regiments in which Sir Francis had served.

Sir Francis died before I went to Rolls Park. Lady Lloyd kept all his uniform beside her bed – the busby and everyday uniform in a case in her bedroom and down in the front hall a big brass screen; because he was in the Grenadier Guards, there was his Dress uniform, all his medals, swords, everything down to his boots. In the front hall were the Grenadier Guards drums – two big drums. Upstairs on the big landing was everything Sir Francis used for his exercises – a bar suspended on two ropes and he used to swing up there. It was all out of the ordinary.

Lady Lloyd had a beautiful bedroom that looked over the park – how she sat there on her own I do not know but she was miles away from the rest of us.

At 10 o'clock [pm] I used to have to go and fetch a dog from the bailiff's cottage – it was a black retriever – I used to have to take him for a walk round the grounds and then he'd go in his basket by the side of Lady Lloyd's bed and he'd stop there for the night and she would also have the Peke on her bed.

Of course, there was the Chinese bedroom and the Japanese bedroom which were furnished in that style – beautiful – and the haunted bedroom which, fortunately, was never used. I never saw any sign of a ghost and I never heard of anyone who did but I wouldn't go down there if I could help it. I didn't know of any legend about it. There was supposed to be a ghost that rode along the top of the wall in a carriage, which always mystified me. I believe people had seen that but I never did and I didn't think anybody did while I was there.

There was a famous Grinling Gibbons staircase and in the park a large cork tree stood. It was very quiet, there wasn't much entertaining. Occasionally at weekends, Lady Lloyd would have friends to stay – mostly elderly ladies like herself and quite a few famous people used to stay now and again. We used to have Mr Winston Churchill. He used to come especially at election time because this was his constituency and he used to come down for meetings round about, he and his wife, a very sweet woman by the way. He was a bit overpowering, but I suppose a man in his position would be.

We used to play cards in the evenings – Miss Roberts, the chauffeur and I. Sometimes, Lady Lloyd would go away to friends and relations and then we were free to do as we liked as long as the place was clean and safe. There was a big bustle before she came back.

She let the house for three months once and went down to Eridge to stay with a brother. She left us to keep an eye on the place. One day they let us have the car and we went to Bradwell-on-Sea in Essex, but it was a small car; the cook was a very big woman and there was about five of us in it. Every time we went round a bend we all had to lean in the opposite direction from the cook to keep the car balanced.

Normally, I was busy doing housework all the morning. Miss Roberts was in the kitchen preparing meals and the kitchen maid was doing her cleaning. She did have a hard time. She had to scrub the stone paving stones and being so old they were all trodden up and down.

We had very good food – not the same as Lady Lloyd – she had a very small appetite and had light meals, but she was fond of bananas cooked in rum. We had plenty of good meat dinners with vegetables that were grown on the estate. Breakfast we always had eggs, bacon, fish, fishcakes, toast and marmalade and, of course tea. At tea time we had bread, jam, eggs and cakes and supper consisted of such things as Shepherds pie and soup. We were very well fed and we always had sausages from Epping on Sundays.

Lady Lloyd's meals were always served on pewter plates. Miss Roberts was instructed never to put them in the oven. One day the meal was ready but she could not find the butler so she put the plate of food in the oven. The dish melted. Next day when Lady Lloyd went to the kitchen, Miss Roberts said 'I'm very sorry m'lady, I've melted the dish'. 'What have I told you?' she said. 'Well, I've been honest with you m'lady. Look on top of your pantry – you'll find many bits of pewter.'

I found Lady Lloyd very kind and she was the only one who worried about my pale cheeks. I remember she said 'I do not like the colour of your face. I've been to see Mr Hutchins (the chemist whose shop still stands today). He has recommended these Dr Williams pink pills for pale people.' I had to take these pills and they made no difference. She bought me one thing after another until in the end she said 'I do not think there is anything more I can buy now except a box of rouge'. (Of course, she didn't buy it and I wouldn't have used it in any case.)

The days were long from half-past six in the morning till ten o'clock at night but we were very happy. I think it was the happiest time of my life. Rolls Park was a beautiful house with the forest and the woods all round and a lovely garden. If one wanted to go for a walk we could take the dogs out in the woods - it was really lovely.

I still go out there to have a peep as I became attached to the place.

18. The decline of Rolls Park 1939–1953

Sir Francis Lloyd spent many thousands of pounds on restoring and maintaining Rolls Park during the time that he owned it and lived at Chigwell and he also had the upkeep of another large house at Aston in Shropshire. The story of the last three decades of the fight to save Rolls was recounted in correspondence between Sir Francis Lloyd's nephew, Andrew Lloyd, who inherited Rolls in 1939, and *Country Life* magazine.

In a letter to *Country Life*, published in the edition of 28 November 1974, Andrew Lloyd explained that:

Rolls Park, Essex, came into my family on the death in 1830 of Admiral Sir Eliab Harvey whose eldest child, Louisa, had already married William Lloyd of Aston in 1804. Thereafter during the 19th century, and well into the 20th, the old house was always let, and rather badly too, because even in those days tenants could not properly afford its upkeep.

Sir Francis Lloyd decided [in c1914] that he would leave Shropshire and go to live at Rolls. He sank many thousands of pounds into the house and eventually took up residence there for the few years that were left to him. When Sir Francis died, my father, a humble country parson, inherited. He secured a let, but very soon he was in trouble over the huge maintenance costs, and despite all the money that had so recently been sunk into the house. There is no doubt in my mind that the Essex country house, unlike its Shropshire or Cotswold counterpart, does suffer certain structural weaknesses.

Then in 1939 came the Second World War. Rolls was immediately taken over by the army. It was while I was waiting a posting overseas that my father died, and I, for my sins, not only became the owner of Rolls, but of Aston too.

During the war, sections of different regiments of troops were to be stationed at Rolls, and it would be difficult indeed for me to describe the damage that they did. They hacked off chunks of the delectable Tudor back staircase until it was barely safe, and they had even started work on the Grinling Gibbons front staircase. Fortunately old Gibbons was just a bit too tough for them, and so in the main his work was preserved. One of the officers in charge whom I met when on leave was sufficiently shocked to suggest that an extensive 'boarding up' should be carried out and though rather late in the day, much was saved in this manner.

While the army was active inside the house, other agents of even greater destruction were more active outside it. Rolls lay some 13 miles north east of London and right on the Luftwaffe's shortest way in. The result was that the immediate area was plastered with ack-ack gun sites containing guns of the largest calibre, and as the barrage went up each night, the poor old house was shaken to its very foundations. Ack-ack guns attract bombs, and though Rolls never had a direct hit, there were many near misses. It is true that the bombs mostly fell on soft ground, but their impact was considerable nevertheless, to say nothing of the V1s and V2s.

One of the V1s circled the house many times until it cleared the old garden wall literally by inches. That wall saved us from the full force of the blast, but the explosion was enough to bring down enormous chunks of masonry and roof. Fortunately the only casualty was a heifer.

I was handed back my shambles soon after the war ended – plus a cheque for £8,000 by way of compensation. I was told at the time that even £50,000 would have gone but a short way towards the work of restoration, and in those days £50,000 was a lot of money.

One day a young man came and visited me. I think he was representing some body interested in the preservation of country houses. He went into great detail as to what I should be doing, and when I ventured to ask him how he thought I could pay for such a monumental work of restoration, when I already had another, even larger mansion on my hands also suffering war damage, he was strangely silent. For once he could make no suggestions.

Meantime, and I am talking about the early 1950s now, an industrial area showed signs of growing up around Rolls,[85] and pilfering became widespread. I think it was this fact that made me finally throw in my hand in 1953 and allow the house to be demolished.

Today all that remains of the original buildings are the Orangery, the Old Cottage and the Stables. However, the grand staircase, which Lloyd attributed to Grinling Gibbons, but may in fact have been by Thomas Kinward, master-joiner to King Charles II, was moved to Hinchingbrooke House, Cambridgeshire, in 1953, where the original staircase, destroyed by fire in 1830, was by Kinward.

19. The Harvey family portraits

During the two hundred years that the Harvey family lived at Rolls Park a remarkable collection of portraits of members of the family were painted by some very well-known artists, including Sir Godfrey Kneller and Thomas Hudson. Many of these portraits remain in the possession of a descendant of the Harvey family and with the Harveian Society of London.

The portraits of Eliab Harvey (1589–1661) and his descendants have been handed down within the families descended from Louisa Harvey and Maria Harvey, the major collection now being at Betchworth, Surrey. The twelve portraits at Betchworth consist of:

Doctor William Harvey (1578-1657)

First son of Thomas and Joan Harvey of Folkestone. Discoverer of the circulation of the blood. Married Elizabeth Browne, but no children.

Artist: Unknown. A copy of a portrait attributed to Cornelius Janssens (1593–1661).

Oils on canvas. 138cm x 107cm. Unsigned.

Three-quarter length. Seated. There are several Janssen portraits of William Harvey. The Betchworth portrait is probably an early nineteenth century copy by an anonymous artist.

Eliab Harvey, Esquire (1589–1661)

Fifth son of Thomas and Joan Harvey, and brother of Doctor William Harvey.

Artist: Sir Peter Lely (1618–1680) or his studio.

Oils on canvas. 122cm x 97cm. Unsigned.

Three-quarter length. Probably painted after 1630 when fashion for the ruff gave way to a plain collar. In the lower right-hand corner there are three letters on a table, one of which is written 'To Mr Eliab Harvey, MT. in London'.

Mary Harvey (1607–1673)
Wife of Eliab Harvey, Esquire (1589–1661). Daughter of Francis West.
Artist: Gerard Soest (1637–1681)
Oils on canvas. 127cm x 97cm. Unsigned.

Three-quarter length, showing Mary Harvey in a mauve dress, holding some flowers. Originally thought to be by Lely, but because of style and colouring attributed to Gerard Soest.

Edward Harvey Esquire, MP (1658–1736)
Grandson of Daniel Harvey (1587–1649), a brother of Doctor William Harvey.
Artist: Sir Godfrey Kneller (1646-1723) or his studio.
Oils on canvas 128cm x 99cm. Unsigned.

Three-quarter length. The painting was originally at Rolls Park, although this Edward Harvey did not live there. Shows Harvey in a brown coat with lace cravat and red cloak.

William Harvey, Esquire, MP (1663–1731)
Son of Sir Eliab Harvey (1635–1698). Married Dorothy Dycer.
Artist: Sir Godfrey Kneller (1646–1723) or his studio.
Oils on canvas. 128cm x 99cm. Unsigned.

Three-quarter length. Shows gentleman in classical dress with red scarf and wearing full brown wig.

Dorothy Harvey (1668–1711)
Wife of William Harvey (1663–1731).
Artist: Sir Godfrey Kneller (1646–1723) or his studio.
Oils on canvas. 72cm x 60cm. Unsigned.
Head and shoulders. Low-neck blue dress, with brown scarf.

William Harvey, Esquire, MP (1714–1763)
Son of William Harvey (1663–1731). Married Emma Skynner of Leytonstone.
Artist: Thomas Hudson (1701–1779)
Oils on canvas. 127cm x 97cm.

Three-quarter length. In blue suit and wearing short blond wig.

Emma Harvey (1732–1767)
Wife of William Harvey (1714–1763). Daughter of Stephen Skynner of Leytonstone, Essex.
Artist: Thomas Hudson (1707–1779)
Oils on canvas. 127cm x 97cm.

Three-quarter length. Ornate blue and white silk dress, decorated with pearls. Holding basket of flowers.

Another portrait, also by Thomas Hudson, virtually identical except for the arrangement of the pearls, was sold by Sotheby's to Agnew's in 1958.

Lieutenant Stephen Harvey (1757–1779)
Son of William Harvey (1714–1763). Brother of Admiral Sir Eliab Harvey. Killed at Saratoga, North America, in 1779 and buried there.
Artist: Unknown
Oils on canvas. 85cm x 70cm.

Three-quarter length. Standing. Army lieutenant's uniform with sword. Wearing short grey wig.

Admiral Sir Eliab Harvey (1758–1830)
Son of William Harvey (1714–1763). Married Lady Louisa Nugent. Distinguished action in the *Temeraire* at Trafalgar. With his death the Harvey male line became extinct.
Artist: Attributed to Lemuel Frances Abbot (1760–1803).
Oils on canvas. 140cm x 108cm. Unsigned.

Almost full length. Standing. Full naval captain's uniform. Holding hat. Decorations: Captain's Trafalgar gold medal; Star of Order of the Bath; Red sash of Order of the Bath.

Since Abbot died in 1803, this portrait may be a copy of an earlier one, with decorations added. The National Maritime Museum appears to have the original, and there is also another copy in private hands.

Maria Harvey (1791–1875)
Daughter of Admiral Harvey (1758–1830). Married Rev William Tower (1789–1847) of Weald Hall, Essex.
Artist: Unknown.
Oils on canvas. 73cm x 60cm.

Half length. Seated. Plain blue dress buttoned to neck. Lace bonnet. Sitter was then a widow, aged about 60.

Captain Harvey Tower (1831–1870)
   Son of Maria Harvey (1791–1875). Captain in the Coldstream Guards. Died unmarried.
   Artist: James Godsell Middleton (fl. 1826–1872)
   Oils on canvas. 71cm x 60cm.
   Half length. Red army officer's uniform.

In addition to the portraits, at Betchworth, three other portraits of members of the family may be mentioned.
   A portrait of Louisa Harvey (1785–1866) has descended to another member of the family:

Louisa Harvey (1785–1866)
   Daughter of Admiral Harvey (1758–1830). Married William Lloyd of Aston.
   Artist: Sir George Hayter (1792–1871)
   Oils on canvas. 200cm x 110cm.
   Painted c1825 when Louisa was about 40.
   Full length. Standing. Dark blue dress. Flowing red scarf.

The Harveian Society of London also has two important portraits of Sir Eliab Harvey (1635–1698) and his wife Dorothy (1638–1698):

Sir Eliab Harvey (1635–1698)
   Son of Eliab Harvey (1589–1661) and Mary Harvey (1607–1673). See Betchworth portraits, above.
   Artist: Sir Godfrey Kneller (1646–1723) or his studio.
   Three-quarter length.

Lady Dorothy Harvey (1638–1725)
   Wife of Sir Eliab (1635–1698). Daughter of Sir Thomas Whitmore.
   Artist: Sir Godfrey Kneller or his studio
   Three-quarter length. Seated.

Rolls Park also contained a number of the earliest portraits of the Harvey family. A tableau on the wall of the large dining room (later the rococo Music room) consisted of portraits (artist unknown, but possibly by Daniel

Mytens) of Thomas Harvey, his seven sons (William, Thomas, John, Daniel, Eliab, Mathew and Michael) and one of his daughters, possibly Ameye. When they were rediscovered in 1948 by Sir Geoffrey Keynes, the portraits of Eliab and Mathew had been stolen. The remaining portraits were removed for safe-keeping to the National Portrait Gallery, they were restored and then hung for 10 years in the Royal College of Physicians, London. They were then returned to their owner Mr Andrew Lloyd (Admiral Sir Eliab and Lady Louisa Harvey's great-great grandson). I have been unable to trace the current owners of these paintings.

Another Rolls Park painting by Sir Godfrey Kneller was of a family group, consisting of a later William Harvey (1689–1742), his wife Mary Harvey (née Williamson) (1686–1761), their three sons: William (1714–1763), Eliab (1716–1769) and Edward (1718–1778), and also Mary Harvey's mother, Mrs Williamson. This painting is now in the reserve collection at Tate Britain.

The McManus Galleries in Dundee have a portrait of Edward Harvey (1718–1778) by Allan Ramsay. This Harvey was the third son of William Harvey (1689–1742). Edward had a distinguished military career. The portrait (127cm x 101.6cm) shows Harvey wearing the yellow-lined red coat of an officer in the 10th Dragoons.

Finally there is also a portrait of Sir Daniel Harvey (1631–1672) by Sir Peter Lely, now owned by Whitgift School, Croydon.

20. The Harvey monuments at Hempstead, Essex

The Harvey connection with Essex started in the north-west part of the county in the village of Hempstead, where, sometime before 1647, Eliab Harvey (1589–1661) or his brother William (1578–1657), purchased the manor of Winchlow (Winslow), and came to live at Winchlow Hall. Although the Harveys retained the estate for 200 years, it appears that, certainly by 1670, their main residence was at Rolls Park, Chigwell.

While living at Winchlow Hall, Eliab had, in 1655, built the north chapel and vestry at the Church of St Andrew in Hempstead. The chapel was built over the vault of the Harvey family which today contains 49 lead coffins of members of the family and on the lids of some, are modelled the likeness of the face of the deceased. The Harvey monuments in the chapel above the vault include:

Eliab Harvey (1589–1661) and members of his family including his son, Sir Eliab Harvey (1635–1699). The large black and white marble monument has a cleft pediment and a cartouche of arms.

William Harvey (1578–1657). There are two monuments, first in the centre of the chapel is a large sarcophagus made from a single block of Carrara marble. It contains the remains of Dr William Harvey, which were placed there by the Royal College of Physicians in 1883. At the east end of the north aisle is a bust of William Harvey which is said to be a very good likeness of him, with one eye slightly larger than the other and traces of former palsy down one side of his face. The sculptor was Edward Marshall.

William Harvey (1692–1742) and his wife Mary. The monument is in grey and white marble with drape-shaded medallions showing their faces in profile. The sculptor was Louis Roubiliac.

William Harvey (1640–1719) and Bridget his wife. A recess contains a huge circular marble plinth, surmounted by a flaming urn. Above is a coat of arms, decorated with garlands of flowers.

Admiral Sir Eliab Harvey (1758–1830). The monument contains details of his naval career and also refers to son William, who died in 1823 at the age of 22 years. Admiral Harvey's hatchment also hangs in the north aisle.

Edward Harvey (1790–1812). A plain black marble tablet in memory of the Captain in the Coldstream Guards who 'fell honourably in the lines of Burgos'.

The oldest parts of the church go back to the fourteenth century (nave arcades) and the chancel windows show the perpendicular architecture of the fifteenth century. The east end was rebuilt in Tudor brick during the early sixteenth century. The church remained structurally unaltered until misfortune struck in 1882 when the fifteenth century tower collapsed – due, it is thought, to weakness and decay in the south-east buttress. The church was restored and reopened in May 1888, but the work of rebuilding the tower did not begin until 1933. The cost of rebuilding was met by the William Harvey Memorial Fund and the Harveian Society of London. However, due to a shortage of funds, work was not completed until 1962.

21. Other Essex connections with Trafalgar

The Parish Church of St Leonard's, Southminster, has a link with Nelson and his famous victory at Trafalgar for, in the vestry, are some items of furniture which were formerly in Nelson's cabin on the *Victory*. They consist of a large table/desk, a bookcase, a fireplace and a mirror.

These items were brought to Southminster by the Rev A J Scott, who was Nelson's chaplain and private secretary, and who was present at the death of the celebrated admiral. In fact it was to Scott that Nelson addressed his last words: 'Thank God I have done my duty.'

Alexander John Scott was born in Rotherhithe in 1768, the son of a lieutenant in the Royal Navy. He was educated at Charterhouse and St John's College, Cambridge. In 1793 he became private secretary to Admiral Sir Hyde Parker. The Rev Scott possessed unusual talents for diplomacy and he mastered several foreign languages. He was a great collector of books and music, which was a rather inconvenient hobby to pursue when serving in one His Majesty's ships.

He was present at the Battle of Copenhagen in 1801, where he was chaplain in HMS *London,* and in 1802 he was presented with the benefice of Southminster, the patrons being the governors of Charterhouse. In 1803 he paid a short visit to Southminster and, in the same year, he became chaplain and private secretary to Lord Nelson in HMS *Victory*, in which capacity he continued until Nelson's death at Trafalgar.

After attending Nelson's funeral at St Paul's, he took up residence at the Vicarage, Burnham-on-Crouch, at the same time also being curate of Southminster. He was much concerned regarding the welfare of the widows and dependants of those who had lost their lives at Trafalgar and he inaugurated a fund for this purpose.

Astronomy was another of the many interests of Mr Scott, and the large wooden sundial which may be seen today on the south wall of the church was erected during his incumbency. In 1816 Scott left Southminster on his appointment as chaplain to the Prince Regent and he was presented to a Government living at Catterick, Yorkshire. The relics from the *Victory* remain in the church at Southminster.[86]

Bibliography

Briggs, N, *Admiral Sir Eliab Harvey, Essex Worthy*. (Notes for lecture at Wansfell College 1977.)
Chelmsford Chronicle.
Country Life, 31 August 1918, 17 January 1957, 28 November 1974.
Dictionary of National Biography.
Erith, E J, *History of Chigwell*, MSS, vols 1 and 2.
Essex Record Office (ERO), Correspondence mainly between Lady Louisa Harvey and her daughter Louisa Lloyd (ref D/DGu).
Essex Journal.
Essex Review.
Essex Union.
Fraser, E, *Famous Fighters of the Fleet* (1904).
Gentleman's Magazine.
Harleian Society, *The Visitations of Essex.*
Hayton, D, *The House of Commons 1690–1715* (2002).
Henning, B, *The House of Commons 1660–1690* (1983).
Holcroft, Sir W, *His Booke.*
Kent and Essex Mercury.
Keynes, G, *The Life of William Harvey.*
Morant, P, *History & Antiquities of Essex* (1768).
Namier & Brooke, *The House of Commons 1754–1790* (1964).
Ogborne, E, *History of Essex* (1815).
Ralfe, *Naval Biographies* (1828).
Royal College of Physicians, Catalogue of exhibition of Portraits (1980).
Royal Commission for Historic Monuments, *Essex*, vols i and ii.
St Andrew's Church, Hempstead, *Guide.*
Sakula, A, *Journal of Royal Naval Medical Service*, vol 65, Winter 1979.
Sakula, A, 'Betchworth Portraits', article in *Medical History* (1981).
Sedgwick, R, *The House of Commons 1715–1754* (1970).
Stott, G, *A History of Chigwell School* (1960).
Thorne, R, *The House of Commons 1790–1820* (1986).
Uden, G, *The Fighting Temeraire* (1961).
Victoria County History of Essex, vol iv.
Wright, T, *The History and Topography of the County of Essex* (1836).

Notes

1. Foster & Green, *History of the Wilmer Family* (1888).
2. ERO: D/DU 97/1.
3. Feet of Fines, Hilary 19 & 20 Chas. II.
4. *Ibid*, Trinity 12 Wm. III.
5. Lay Subsidies, 108/247.
6. Archd. Essex, 95 Stephyn.
7. Lay Subsidies, 111/514, 517.
8. *Ibid*, 112/617.
9. Chanc. Proc., Chas. I, BB 67/13.
10. Close Roll, 15 Chas. I, xxii, 5; 16 Chas. I, xvii, 34.
11. Royalist Composition Papers, Ser. I, vii, 397, 400, 403.
12. Lay Subsidies, 246/19.
13. RCHM, *Essex*, ii, p48.
14. ERO, Q/RTh.
15. Cal SP, Dom, 1667/8, 72.
16. *Ibid*, Addenda 1660–70, 729.
17. *Ibid*, 1670, 617.
18. Hayton, D, *The House of Commons 1690–1715* (2002).
19. Essex Record Office: D/DCv 3/10.
20. Hayton, D, *op cit*, note 18.
21. Court of Attachments, 1/1, 1/71, 2/59.
22. Erith, *History of Chigwell*, MSS, vol. 1, p 170.
23. Hayton, D, *op cit*, note 18.
24. Erith, *op cit*, note 22, vol 2.
25. ERO, Q/R Hi 1/7.
26. Hayton, D, *op cit*, note 18.
27. *Gentleman's Magazine*, xx, 88.
28. (Gilly Williams to George Selwyn), Jesse (John Heneage), *George Selwyn and His Contemporaries*, i, 226 (1843).
29. Royal Society Archives.
30. *Journal of the Reign of George III, 1771–83*, Ed. Doran, vol 1, p 179.
31. J Eyre to R Newdigate, 13 Oct 1775, Newdigate MSS.
32. ERO, Q/S Mg 2.
33. *Gentleman's Magazine*, xcii (Pt 2) 285.
34. Chancellor, W, *Essex Archaeological Society Trans.*, NS xii (1913).
35. *Ibid*.
36. *Harrow School Registers, 1571–1800*, Ed W T J Gun (1934).
37. ERO: T/B 251/4/1.
38. *Ibid*, Letter dated 5 December 1780.
39. ERO: T/B 251/4/2.
40. *English Chronicle* 1781.
41. ERO: T/B 251/4/3, Letter dated 21 December 1783.
42. *Ibid*, Letter dated 24 December 1783.
43. ERO: T/B 251/4/4, Letter dated 22 January 1784.
44. National Library of Wales, Aston Hall MSS 453, 7197.
45. Caunt, G, 'Political Quartette', *Essex Journal*, April 1970.
46. ERO: D/DGu Z1.
47. This is a mistake, both ships were French.
48. Annual Register, x/vii, 236.
49. ERO: D/DGu C8.
50. Sakula, A, 'Admiral Sir Eliab Harvey of the Temeraire: A Distinguished Kinsman of William Harvey', in *Journal of the Royal Naval Medical Service*, vol 65 (3) (1979).
51. ERO: D/DGu C2/1/1.
52. *Ibid*.

53. *Ibid.*
54. There is no documentary evidence for this, although timber from Hainault Forest was a source of supply for the Navy.
55. Sakula, A, *op cit,* note 50.
56. National Maritime Museum, ref PBD 3139.
57. The table and chairs were originally in St Paul's Church, Rotherhithe, which adjoined Beatson's shipbreaker's yard. The Church was demolished in c1970.
58. Sakula, A, *op cit,* note 50.
59. Ralfe, *Naval Biographies,* ii, 434.
60. *Gentleman's Magazine,* lxxix, 472.
61. *Ibid*, lxxx (Pt 2) 182.
62. *Essex Union,* 30 March, 1810.
63. *Ibid,* 27 Oct., 1809.
64. *Ibid,* 16 Mar., 1810.
65. *Chelmsford Chronicle,* 19 June 1818.
66. ERO: D/DGu C2/1/7.
67. ERO: D/DGu C2/1/6.
68. *Kent and Essex Mercury,* 6 May 1823.
69. *Ibid,* 13 July 1824.
70. *Ibid,* 28 Feb 1826.
71. *Ibid,* 30 Oct 1827.
72. *Ibid,* 17 March 1829.
73. ERO: D/DGu Z1.
74. *Kent and Essex Mercury,* 23 Feb 1830.
75. *Ibid,* 23 March 1830.
76. ERO: D/DGu C3/1/2.
77. ERO: D/DGu C4/1/4.
78. *Kent and Essex Mercury,* 3 April 1832.
79. ERO: D/DGu C3/1/1.
80. ERO: D/DGu C3/1/1.
81. *Ibid.*
82. *Ibid.*
83. ERO: D/CT 78.
84. Now the Loughton and District Historical Society.
85. This is probably a reference to the Debden estate, a mile away from Rolls in Loughton Parish.
86. Sherlock, J W, *Essex Review,* lvii, 173–177 (1948).

APPENDIX

Pedigree of the Harvey Family

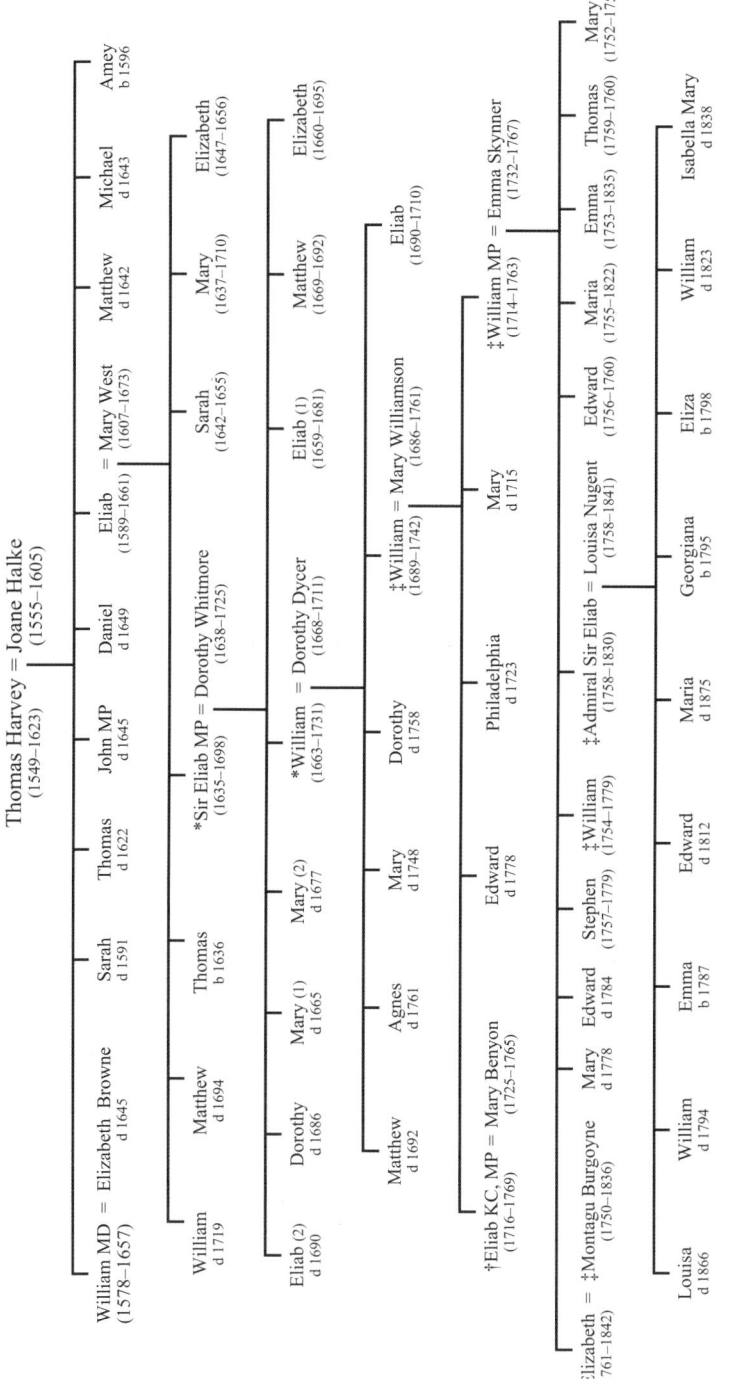

‡ Verderer of Waltham Forest
* Lieutenant of Waltham Forest
† Steward of the Court of Attachments

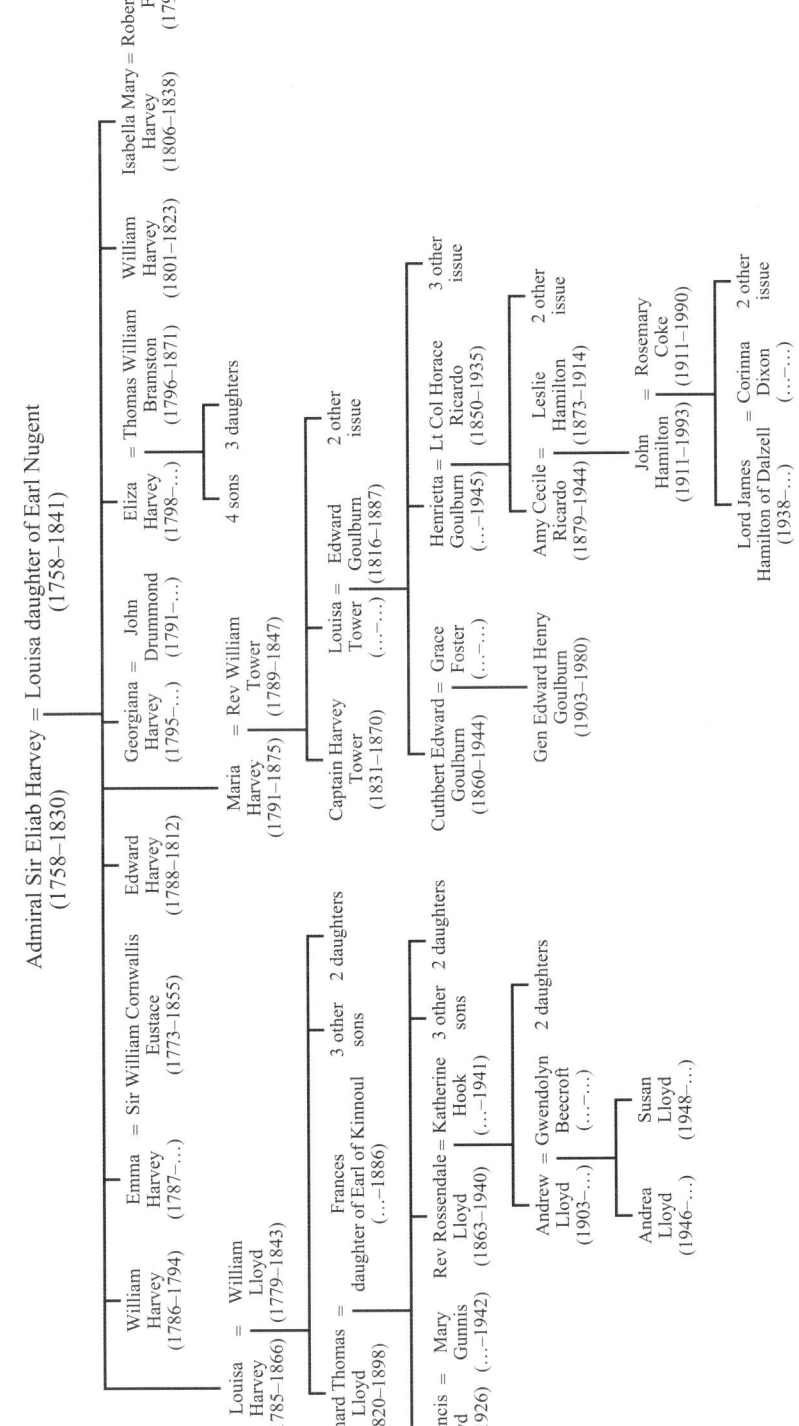

LOUGHTON AND DISTRICT HISTORICAL SOCIETY

Publications List

Transactions No 1 (1970)*: ISBN 9028 9300 9, £1
Transactions No 2 (1974): ISBN 9028 9300 7, £1
Pohl, D J: *Loughton 1851 – the Village and its People* (1988)*: ISBN 9028 9302 5, £3
Elliott, B: *History of the Loughton and Chigwell Police* (1991): ISBN 9028 9303 3, £2
Russell, V J and Dare, E H: *A Walk Round Chigwell* (1992), 75p
Ambrose, P: *Reminiscences of a Loughton Life* (1995)*: ISBN 0952 53440 1, £5.25
Paar, H W: *Loughton's First Railway Station* (1996)*: ISBN 0952 88050 4, £3.50
Hunter, R, Elliot, W H and Pond, C C: *The Life of Robert Hunter 1823–1897, Lexicographer, Missionary, Geologist and Naturalist* (1997)*: ISBN 0952 88051 2, £5
Pond, C C: *History of the Loughton Methodist Church and of Methodist Expansion in SW Essex* (1998): ISBN 0952 88052 0, £4
Whiting, A: *The Loughton Roding Estate, From Cattle-Grazing to Double-Glazing* (1998): ISBN 0952 88053 9, £3
Wilkinson, D: *From Mean Streets to Epping Forest: The Shaftesbury Retreat, Loughton* (2000): ISBN 0952 88054 7, £3
Waller, W C [Pond, C C, Ed]: *Notes on Loughton 1890-95* (2001): ISBN 0952 88056 3, £1.50
Morris, R S: *William Chapman Waller 1850-1917: Loughton's Historian* (hardbound book with 16 pages of colour plates) (2001)*: ISBN 0952 88055 5, £7.50
Morris, R S and Pond, C C (Eds)*: *Loughton a Hundred Years Ago* (2001): ISBN 0952 88057 1, £5.50
Pond, C C: *A Walk Round Loughton* (2002), £1.25
Waller, W C [Morris, R S, Ed]: *Notes on Loughton – II: 1896-1914* (2002): ISBN 0952 88059 8, £2.00
Lockington, E and Trickey, W: *The Coffee House at Woodford* (2002): ISBN 0954 2314 1 4, £5
Pond, C and C: *Walks in Loughton's Forest* (2002): ISBN 0954 2314 0 6, £3
Woodhouse, Peter: *Life in Loughton 1926–46* (2003): ISBN 0954 2314 5 7, £5
Pond, C C: *The Buildings of Loughton and Notable People of the Town* (2003): ISBN 0954 2314 3 0, £5
Morris, R S: *The Powells in Essex and their London Ancestors* (hardbound book with 16 pages of colour plates) (2003): ISBN 0954 2314 2 2, £9.50
Morris, R S: *The Verderers and Courts of Waltham Forest in the County of Essex 1250–2000* (hardbound book with 16 pages of colour plates) (2004): ISBN 0954 2314 6 5, £14.95
Green, Gertrude [Pond, C C, Ed]: *My Life in Loughton* (2004): ISBN 0954 2314 7 3, £5
Morris, R S: *The Harveys of Rolls Park, Chigwell, Essex* (2004): ISBN 0954 2314 9 X, £5

Books are softbound except those indicated as hardbound, above. Titles marked * are out-of-print, or only a few copies are left in stock. Items can be had by post (cash with order – cheques payable to Loughton and District Historical Society) from Forest Villa, Staples Road, Loughton, Essex, IG10 1HP at the prices given – post free in the UK, cash with order. For post abroad, with payment in dollars or other currencies, please write or e-mail (Loughton_Ponds@hotmail.com) first. Overseas postage charged at cost.

10 per cent discount on direct sales to schools, libraries and record offices. Books sent on invoice after official order.